Gracious, Most Merciful

Biblical Children's Stories

As Told in

The Qur'an

Narrated by Susan Smith
Illustrated by Anahita Taymourian

Published by

Tahrike Tarsile Qur'an, Inc.

Publishers and Distributors of the Holy Qur'an
80-08 51st Avenue
Elmhurst, New York 11373
E-Mail: read@koranusa.org
http://www.koranusa.org

Sept. 27, 2017

Dear Jane,

Thank you so much to you and the Presbyterian Women of Newton Presbytery for inviting me to speak about refugees.

May God bless, protect and sustain you all in your continued good work.

Love and peace,

Susan

Dedicated to
Yasmine and Dareen,
and children everywhere.
May we love one another always.

Published by
TahrikeTarsile Qur'an, Inc.
Publishers and Distributors of the Holy Qur'an
80-08 51st Avenue
Elmhurst, New York 11373-4141
www.koranusa.org
E-mail: read@koranusa.org

First U.S. Edition 2015
Library of Congress Catalog Number: 2010940344
British Library Cataloguing in Publication Data
ISBN: 978-1-879402-61-4

Susan Smith

A convert to Islam since 1986, Susan Smith, belongs to Stony Point Center's Community of Living Traditions, an intentional multi-faith community committed to universal human rights and non-violence. Stony Point is a conference and retreat center catering to peace and social justice groups and is operated by the Presbyterian Church USA in New York.

Ms. Smith is a former Islamic school principal who has worked at the United Nations in various capacities including: UN liaison for Islamic Relief USA; information officer with the UN's Department of Public Information, voter registration officer on a UN Peace-keeping Mission in the Western Sahara; and as assistant and speech-writer to the ambassador of Lebanon and president of the UNICEF ExecutiveBoard.

Ms. Smith has a Masters Degree in Educational Counseling and Development from Long Island University and a Masters Diploma in Middle East Studies from the American University in Cairo. She has lived, worked, studied and traveled extensively in the Middle East, and has a deep and abiding love for the people of that region. She resided in the Holy City of Jerusalem in 1986 and performed the Hajj to Mecca in 2009.

AnahitaTaymourian

AnahitaTaymourian is a university lecturer, graphic artist, painter, interior designer and internationally-acclaimed illustrator. She has a Master's of Science in Architecture and Painting and was born in Tehran, Iran in 1972.

Among her extensive list of publications are: The Kid of All published by BohemPress, Switzerland, 2008; Kaleh and the Singsong Castle published by Katha Books, India, 2007; Sami's Fear of Nights and My Sweetie, Sara published Alvita Publishing Company, Taiwan, 2006; My Moon, Our Moon published by Commercial Press, Ltd., Taiwan, 2004 and Shinseken Ltd., Japan, 2003; and The Moon and the Fox published by the Institute for the Intellectual Development of Children and Young Adults, Iran, 2000.

Ms. Taymourian has achieved numerous distinctions as a children's book illustrator. She was runner-up in the international search for excellence and innovation in illustrating and writing for children at the Katha Chitrakala Awards, India, 2005; selected for outstanding artistry at the International Illustration Competition in Teatrio, Italy, 2005; winner at the International Illustration Competition in Teatrio, Italy, 2004; and runner-up at the NomaConcours for Picture Book Illustrations, Japan, 2000.

Table of Contents

May God's peace and blessings be upon all the Prophets

In the Name of God, the Most Beneficent, the Most Merciful,

All praise and thanks are God's, the Lord of the worlds,

The Most Gracious, the Most Merciful,

The Only Owner of the Day of Recompense,

You (Alone) we worship, and You (Alone) we ask for help,

Guide us to the Straight Way,

The Way of those on whom You have bestowed Your Grace,

not (the way) of those who earned Your anger,

nor of those who went astray.

The Qur'an, Chapter One: The Opening

Foreword

Islamic narration tells us that God sent 124 thousand Prophets to mankind. These were wise men sent to humanity at different times and places to communicate His Message. They were chosen to teach those around them about the One True God. By following their examples, we learn to live our lives in the manner which pleases Him.

And for every nation there is a Messenger.
The Qur'an, Chapter 10, Jonah, Verse 47

And certainly We raised in every nation a Messenger, saying:
Serve God and shun the devil.
The Qur'an, Chapter 16, The Bee, Verse 36

Of these, 25 Prophets are mentioned in the Qur'an. Each was instructed to guide his people to the path of love, light and goodness.

Say: We believe in God, and in what has been revealed to us and
what was revealed to Abraham, Ishmael, Isaac, Jacob, and the Tribes, and in
that which was given to Moses and Jesus and the Prophets, from their Lord.
We make no distinction between one and another among them
and we submit to Him. If anyone desires a religion other than
submission to the Almighty God, never will it be accepted of him;
and in the Hereafter he will be one of the losers."
The Qur'an, Chapter 3 The Family of Imraan, Verses 84-85

Some Prophets delivered God's Word through books of Revelation. These are the Sheets of Abraham, the Torah of Moses, the Psalms of David, the Gospels of Jesus, and the Qur'an as revealed to Muhammad. These five

Prophets are considered Messengers of God. However, only Muhammad delivered a Revelation to all of humanity rather than a specific population.

God has revealed (from time to time) the most beautiful Message in the form of a Book, consistent with itself yet repeating (its teaching in various aspects). The skins of those who fear their Lord tremble at that, and then their skins and their hearts soften to the celebration of God's praises. Such is the guidance of God: He guides therewith whom He pleases...
The Qur'an, Chapter 39, The Crowds, Verse 23

He has ordained for you of religion what He enjoined upon Noah and that which We have sent by inspirationand that which We enjoined upon Abraham, Moses and Jesus:to establish the religion and not be divided therein. Those who worship other than God, hard is the way which you call them. God chooses for Himself those whom He pleases and guides to Him.

The same religion He has established for you as that which He enjoined on Noah that which We have sent by inspiration to you those who turn (to Him).
The Qur'an, Chapter 42, The Consultation, Verse 13

Adam

In the history of mankind, Adam was not only the first human being, but the first Prophet. God created him from black clay and breathed life into him after 40 days. Then God created his wife, Eve (Hawa), and they lived in paradise, which was more pristine and comfortable than we can imagine. They lived in ultimate bliss their only responsibility was to worship and obey God, Who said:

Oh Adam, live with your wife in the garden of paradise, and eat whatever and as much as you want. However, don't go near the forbidden tree or you will be in trouble!
The Qur'an, Chapter 2, The Cow, Verse 35

Meanwhile, God had commanded Satan to bow down to Adam, but he refused. In his anger and jealously, Satan decided to trick Adam and Eve into disobeying God. He told them that if they ate from the forbidden tree, they would live forever. Eventually, Adam and Eve believed Satan's lies and ate from the tree.

God was furious and said, "Both of you leave here!
Get down from the garden of paradise despising each other!
However, when I give guidance, which I surely will,
*whoever follows it will not lose his way or be miserable.*The Qur'an, Chapter 20, Ta Ha, Verse 123

So Adam and Eve were cast out of paradise and banished to earth, where they had to work and struggle for everything. Lost and miserable, they begged for God's mercy and guidance. He forgave them because they were truly sorry, but did not allowed them to return to Paradise. God told them that from that day forward, they would be relegated to earth until the Day of Judgment. They would be allowed to return to paradise if they demonstrated righteous conduct on Earth.

What is righteous conduct, one might ask? How do we get to paradise? God, the Merciful and the Compassionate, made this clear: Worship Him and follow the teachings of His Prophets.

Adam was the first Prophet sent to mankind. After him, God dispatched many others to complete His Message and disseminate it to all people throughout the lands.

Enoch (Idris)

The Prophet Enoch was born 100 years after the death of Prophet Adam. He was the first man who learned to write and the inventor of astronomy and arithmetic. It is said that thirty portions of God's sacred scriptures were revealed to him.

> *...Indeed, (Enoch) was a man of truth and a Prophet,*
> *and We raised him to a lofty station.*
> The Qur'an, Mary, Chapter 19, Verse 56

As the history of the human race did unfold, some of Adam's descendants began associating idols with God and worshipping statues. Moreover, many abandoned the teachings of Adam and began to lie, cheat, steal, get drunk on wine, and engage in debauchery. God, in His mercy, sent the Prophet Enoch to guide them..

Enoch reminded his people to practice monotheism, which is the belief in the One True God. He implored them to abandon idol worship and give up their evil ways. He advised them not abandon the love of wealth and property, and to abstain from drinking wine. A few paid heed, but the majority did not.

In spite of his efforts to preach God's message, Enoch gained few followers and became disheartened. God directed him to migrate to Egypt, where he settled on the banks of the Nile River. There, he preached to many tribes and instilled morality in the people of Egypt, who are known today for their kindness and devotion.

Prophet Enoch died at the age of 365, when his guardian angel escorted him up into the heavens. When they arrived in the fourth heaven, they met the Angel of Death. The guardian angel asked the Angel of Death how many years were left in Prophet Enoch's life, to which the Angel of Death responded, "I have been commanded to end his life." Enoch then died embraced in the wings of his angel friend and he remains today in the fourth heaven.

Noah (Nuh)

Noah was a descendant of Adam born into a generation of sinners. He tried to teach his people to worship and obey God, but they laughed at him. Sometimes they even would hurl stones at him. He complained to God that his people were becoming increasingly disobedient, who commanded:

Warn your people before there comes to them a terrible punishment.
The Qur'an, Chapter 71, Noah, Verse 1

Still, they continued to sin and mock Noah, so God instructed him to build the ark. When they saw him building it far from the sea, they laughed. When it was ready, Noah told those who believed:

Climb into the ark, in the name God,
whether it moves or rests, for my Lord is most forgiving and most merciful.
The Qur'an, Chapter 27, Heber, Verse 41

Soon after, water started pouring from the skies and gushing forth from the seas and rivers. All of the disbelievers were drowned in the great flood, including one of Noah's sons, who had refused to embark. For many days, the vessel tossed about on the colossal waves whilst its passengers prayed for dry land and salvation.

Eventually, God answered their prayers. He decreed the rain to stop, the earth to swallow up the water, and the ark to land on Mount Jodi. Noah and the believers threw themselves on the ground and prostrated themselves in prayers of gratitude to their Lord. They praised Him and thanked Him for His mercy, and asked Him to guide them in all that they were about to do on the clean, new earth.

All in all, Noah preached the Message of God for 950 years, before he passed away. Nonetheless, as days and years went by, the survivors of the deluge and their descendants began to drift astray. God said:

After Noah, We sent many Prophets to their peoples.
They brought clear proofs of God, but they would not believe what they already rejected before. Like this, We close the hearts of the sinners.
The Qur'an, Chapter 10, Jonah, Verse 74

Heber (Hud)

Some four generations after Noah, among the gardens and springs of ancient Yemen, there lived the arrogant people of 'Ad. They were a rich and industrious nation, who built large beautiful houses and towers on every mountain. However, worse than being pompous and boastful, the people of 'Ad committed the greatest sin of all: they worshipped idols.

Among them, there lived the Prophet Heber, who said:

> *Oh my people! Worship God! You have no god but God. Will you not fear Him? Certainly you have invented lies (your other gods).*
> The Qur'an, Chapter 11, Heber, Verse 50

But the leaders of the disbelievers called Heber a lunatic and a liar, to which he replied:

> *Oh my people! I am not a fool, but a Prophet from the Lord and Cherisher of the worlds!*
> The Qur'an, Chapter 7, The Heights, Verses 65-67

Still, they refused to believe Heber and challenged him to bring the wrath of God upon them. At his Lord's behest, he called his followers together and they fled the land of 'Ad. Soon after, a gargantuan black cloud consumed the sky and a ferocious hurricane descended upon the city obliterating it. Today, all that remains of the once rich and powerful nation are a few large stones: a portent of the temporary world in which we live and what awaits in the afterlife.

Shaloh (Salih)

Once upon a time, in the deserts of Jordan, lived the people of Thamud. Their houses were carved into mountain-sides of pink rock and shale.Their land was abundant with springs of cool, crisp water, which fed gardens bearing dates, bananas and oranges. The branches of these trees dripped with fruit and nearly broke from their weight. These riches gave the people a false sense of security, which manifested as boastful pride and arrogance.

Moreover, the people of Thamud were not thankful for their wealth: nor did they praise God. Instead, they worshipped idols. They were callous to the poor and refused to let their animals graze on common land. This angered God, Who had placed the Prophet Shaloh among them. Shaloh said:

Oh my people! Worship God. You have no other god but Him.
Now there has come to you a clear sign from your Lord!
This female camel of God is a sign to you, so leave her to graze in God's earth
and let her come to no harm or you will be seized by a terrible punishment.
The Qur'an, Chapter 7, The Heights, Verse 73

Shaloh reminded them of the riches God had given them, and warned that a harsh punishment awaited if they persisted in their evil deeds. He told them about the ominous fate of the people of 'Ad, to which Thamud's leaders paid no heed and continued worshipping idols as their forefathers did.

God showed them a miracle by revealing a big camel from a mountain, together with its baby, and commanded them not to harm nor kill it.Rather than obey Him and let them graze peacefully, they did a very cruel thing. They ham-strung the she-camel and left her to die.

After defying God's command, they taunted the Prophet even further:

Oh Shaloh, so bring us the punishment you warned about,
*or we will not believe that you are the Prophet of God!*The Qur'an, The Heights, Verse 77

Three days later, Shaloh and a few righteous companions fled the city and God delivered His punishment. Under cover of night as Thamud slept, He struck it with calamitous earthquakes sparing no one. The once magnificent city was left in ruins never to flourish again. What lingers, however, is the whisper of Shaloh's admonition echoing through its rocky remains:"Oh my people, I warned you!"

Abraham (Ibrahim)

Who can be better in religion than one who submits his whole self to God,
does good, and follows the way of Abraham, the true in Faith?
For God did take Abraham for a friend.
The Qur'an, Chapter 4, The Women, Verse 125

Abraham was a great Prophet, who grew up in the cradle of civilization in what is known today as the city of Ur in Iraq. The people of Ur worshipped idols and, in fact, Abraham came from a family of idol makers. He thought this was foolish and said: "Do you really believe these idols are gods? If you do, then you and your people are wrong." Still, while he knew idol worship was ridiculous, he pondered the true nature of God.

One evening, Abraham saw a bright star in the sky and said, "That is my God!" Then, as the star faded away, he realized that it could not be God. Another night, Abraham saw the moon shining brightly in the sky, and he said. "That is my God!" But as the moon disappeared, he realized that it could not be God. Later, he saw the sun rising at dawn and said, "That must be my God, because it is the biggest and brightest thing in the sky." But, when sunset came and the sun disappeared, he realized once more that an object could not be God. Only God is God. Only God is the Creator of the stars, the sun and the moon. Only He is the Master of the universe. With this new surge of clarity and faith, Abraham declared:

Oh my people, I am free from your guilt of worshipping gods other than God!
I firmly and truly turn my face to Him, Who created the heavens and the
earth, and I shall never attribute partners to God!
The Qur'an, Chapter 6, The Cattle, Verses 78-79

He urged the people to make the same declaration - that there is only One God and that they would worship Him alone. However, even those men and women who believed him would not give up their idols, saying "Our fathers and our fathers' fathers worshipped them, so we must do the same."

This angered and worried Abraham, so he devised a plan. When no one was around, he took an axe and smashed the idols to pieces, except the biggest one of all. Then, he put the axe on its shoulder. When the people discovered their broken idols, they became furious and cried "Who has done this to our gods?" They remembered Abraham had insulted their idols and asked him, "Are you the one who did this to our gods?" He pointed to the largest idol and replied, "Look at the axe on his shoulder. Why don't you ask him?"

At this, some of the pagans felt ashamed, because the truth was apparent. Their statues had no power at all: they could neither help nor harm them. This humiliated and enraged them even more, and they took revenge by building a humongous bonfire and catapulting Abraham into it. To this God commanded:

O fire! Be cool and safe for Abraham.
The Qur'an, Chapter 21, The Prophets, Verse 69

Prophet Abraham would have died in the inferno, but his fall into the blaze was as descending into a cool garden. In fact, he found the flames remarkably comfortable. In their midst, he glorified and praised God. His heart was full of love for the Creator. Still, he knew that once the fire burned out, the idol worshippers would despise him even more. Thus, when the blaze died down, he escaped from Iraq and traveled to Palestine, Egypt and Arabia.

Later, when Abraham had reached old age, God gave him a great test. While in Mecca, Angel Gabriel came to him inadream with a Message from God that he must sacrifice Ishmael, who was his only child at the time. Abraham was devastated, but knew that God had given him a command. Even little Ishmael understood that his father must obey God and said, "Oh my father! Do as you are told!"

So, full of sorrow, Abraham prepared to kill his son. He took a sharp knife to Ishmael's neck and began to slice his throat, but it would not penetrate his skin!!! Then, the Angel Gabriel appeared and said, "You have shown your good intentions and obeyed God's orders. This is enough."

Abraham and Ishmael were overjoyed. They praised their Lord and He sent them a ram and commanded them to sacrifice it instead, which they shared with family, friends and the poor. This occasion is observed by Muslims each year with the Celebration of the Sacrifice. During this feast, we thank God for His mercy and all that He has given us. Muslims who perform the Hajj Pilgrimage slaughter animals on this day and distribute the meat to the needy.

Later, when Ishmael was an adult, he and his father built the Ka'aba in Mecca, at the site where Prophet Adam used to pray. This place of worship had been damaged by flood during the time of Prophet Noah. When they rebuilt it on the same foundation they prayed:

Our Lord! Accept this service from us, for You are the All-Hearing and All-Knowing. Our Lord! Make us Muslims bowing to Your will
and show us our places for ritual celebration, and turn to using mercy for You are the Oft-Returning, Most Merciful.
The Qur'an, Chapter 2, The Cow, Verses 127-128

The Message of God as taught to Abraham was written on scrolls, but their whereabouts are unknown today. Nonetheless, God reminds us to follow the teachings of the Prophets:

...the most unfortunate ones will enter the great Hellfire, in which they will neither die nor live. But those who purify themselves will prosper, and glorify the name of their Lord and lift their hearts in prayer. Beware, if you prefer the life of this world,when the Hereafter is better and more enduring.
And this is in the Books of the earliest Revelations,
The Books of Abraham and Moses.
The Qur'an, Chapter 87, The Most High, Verses 12-19

Lot (Lut)

A long time ago, in what is now the Kingdom of Jordan, there lived the wicked and decadent people of Sodom and Gomorrah. God sent Prophet Abraham's nephew Lot to guide them, but few took heed.

And (We sent) Lot, who said to his people:
"What! Do you commit indecencies, which no one in the world
did before you?"
The Qur'an, Chapter 7, The Heights, Verse 80

Moreover, they harassed Lot constantly and even challenged him to bring a curse upon them. They said:

Bring us the Wrath of God if you are telling the truth."
The Qur'an, Chapter 29, The Spider, Verse 29

Hearing that, Lot was at a loss andaskedGod for direction saying:

Oh my Lord! Help me against people who do mischief!
The Qur'an, Chapter 29, The Spider, Verse 30

Then, one day, Lot had visitors and he feared that the evil people of Sodom and Gomorrah would try to harm them. To his surprise, the visitors were not afraid. They informed him that they were sent by God to tell him to gather his family and leave town under the cover of darkness. They warned that those who remained or looked back would perish.

Lot recognized at once that the visitors were angels and followed their directions. However, soon after leaving, his wife insisted on turning back in spite of the angels' warnings and her husband's pleas.

So We rescued him and his family, except for his wife,
who was one of those who stayed behind.
And we rained down on them a shower of brimstone.
Then see the fate of those who indulge in sin and crime!
The Qur'an, Chapter 7, The Heights, Verses 83-84

Today, on the east bank of the Dead Sea, little more than brimstone remains where Sodom and Gomorrah once stood and the body of Lot's wife was reduced to ash and salt.

Ishmael (Ismail)

The Prophet Ishmael was the eldest son of the Prophet Abraham and his second wife Hajar. As he had no children from his first wife Sarah, he married Hajar, who was a pious woman. He did this with Sarah's consent and they prayed to God to bless him with a son.

Abraham said: My Lord! Grant me a righteous child. So We gave him
the good news of a boyready to suffer and be patient
The Qur'an, Chapter 37, Those Arranged by Their Ranks, Verses 100-101

Shortly after Ishmael was born, God commanded Abraham to leave the baby and his mother in Mecca. At that time, Mecca was a desolate place with little trace of life in any form. Thus, he left them in the care of God with just a bag of dates and a skin full of water. With heavy heart he said:

"Oh Lord ! I have made some of my off-spring settle in this barren
valley near the Sacred House so that they may keep up prayer"
The Qur'an, Chapter 14, Abraham, Verse 37

As Prophet Abraham set off to visit Sarah, Hajar ran after him imploring him to take pity on her and Ishmael. No food or water was available and he replied that this is what God commanded him to do. Her response was acceptance and she said, "then God will cause us no harm," and she let him go without resistance. When Abraham was out of sight, she turned in the direction of the Ka'aba and prayed to God for His care and protection.

Shortly thereafter, Hajar and Ishmael's water ran out and their thirst became unbearable. Hajar did what she could to feed the baby, but became increasingly weak. As days passed, her milk ran dry and she could feed him no more.

Ishmael's pangs of hunger turned into painful screams, which Hajar could not bear. With newfound energy, she pulled herself to her feet and began running back and forth between the hills of Safa and Marwa in search of water. She ran seven times from hill to hill when, suddenly, she stopped. There was Ishmael kicking the ground when all of a sudden water miraculously gushed forth! Ishmael and Hajar drank from the ZamZam spring and she resumed suckling her baby. God had saved them from the torture of thirst!

In the days to come, news spread about the abundance of water in the midst of the dry and desolate desert. People traveled from far and wide to the spot where Ishmael and his mother had settled, and the city of Mecca was established as the birthplace of Islam.

We made the House a place of assembly for men and a place of security;
and take as your place of worship the place where Abraham stood to pray.
And We made a covenant with Abraham and Ishmael by saying:
Purify My House for those who visit it and those who meditate therein,
and for those who bow down and prostrate themselves in prayer.
The Qur'an, Chapter 2, The Cow, Verse 125

As years passed, the descendants of Abraham and Ishmael settled as tribes throughout the Arabian Peninsula. One of them was the tribe of Quraysh, into which the Prophet Muhammad, peace be upon him, was born and to whom the final Revelation of the Qur'an was revealed.

Issac (Ishaq)

Issac was Ishmael's brother, miraculously born to Abraham's wife Sarah when she was an old woman, and she and Abraham had all but lost hope that they would ever have a child together. After Abraham proved his complete submission to the orders of God by trying to sacrifice Ishmael, God blessed him with another son. Issac's story demonstrates the importance of keeping the Message of God alive from generation to generation, and of spreading the Revelation to new lands and people.

And We bestowed on him Isaac and, as an additional gift,
(a grandson) Jacob, and We made righteous men of them.
And We made them leaders guiding (people) by Our command.
And We sent them Revelations to do good deeds, to establish regular prayer,
and to give regular charity, and Us (alone) did they serve.
The Qur'an, The Prophets, Verses 72-73

Thus, while Prophet Ishmael lived in Mecca in the Arabian Peninsula, the Prophet Isaac lived in the land of Canaan, north of Egypt and west of Iraq. Like his father, Isaac lived in a tent surrounded by the tents of his people. The land was rich, beautiful and fertile, and he had flocks of sheep and herds of cattle.

However, not all of Abraham's descendants would obey their Lord. His grandson Jacob became a Prophet, but somefollowed in the way of the wicked, worshipped idols, and lost all knowledge of God.

We gave him the good news of Isaac, a Prophet among the righteous,
and We blessed him and Isaac:
but some of their offspring will do right and some
will clearly do wrong to their own souls."
The Qur'an, Those Arranged in Ranks, Verses 112-113

Jacob (Yaqub)

Like his ancestors, the Prophet Jacob was committed to worshipping one God and was in the company of the elect and the good. He continued the legacy of submission to God, taught by his father, Isaac, and grandfather, Abraham.

*Behold! When his (Abraham's) Lord said to him: Submit yourself to My will (be a Muslim)." He (Abraham) said: "I have submitted myself (as a Muslim) to the will of the Lord of the Worlds". And this was the legacy that Abraham left to his sons, and so did Jacob (who said); "Oh my sons! God has chosen the Faith for you. Then die not except in the Faith of submission to the will of the Almighty God*The Qur'an, Chapter 2, The Cow, Verses 131-132

Indeed, Jacob remained a steadfast and obedient servant of God until his dying days.

Or were you witnesses when death visited Jacob, when he said to his sons, "What will you serve after me?" They said, "We will serve your God and the God of your fathers, Abraham and Ishmael and Isaac, one God only, and to Him do we submit."
The Qur'an,Chapter 2, The Cow, Verse133

Jacob was the forefather of the 12 tribes of Israel, named after his sons: Asher, Dan, Gad, Issachar, Judah, Levi, Naphtali, Reuben, Simeon, Zebulun, Benjamin and Joseph. Among them, Joseph, his best and most beloved son, was also a Prophet.

Joseph (Yusuf)

Joseph came from a direct line of Prophets. He was the son of Jacob, the grandson of Isaac, and the great-grandson of Abraham. Not only was he blessed with the righteous character of one raised among generations of Prophets, he was amazingly handsome as well – one of the best-looking men that ever lived.

In fact, Joseph was so good, smart and handsome that his brothers hated him. They were jealous that Joseph behaved in a manner as if he could see God, and that he always tried to please God, thereby winning the adoration of their father.

One morning, the sun appeared over the horizon, bathing the earth in its glory. Joseph awoke from his sleep excited by a dream he had had, and ran to tell Jacob.

Oh my father!
Verily, I saw (in a dream) eleven planets and the sun and the moon.
I saw them prostrating themselves to me.
The Qur'an, chapter 12, Joseph, Verse 4

His father's face lit up. Now, he was sure that Joseph would be the one to fulfill the prophecy of his grandfather, Prophet Abraham, and keep the light of God's Message to mankind alive. However, he knew Joseph's brothers would be jealous, so he warned him not to tell them his dream.

O my son! Relate not your vision to your brothers,
lest they arrange a plot against you.
Verily! Satan is to man an open enemy!

Thus will your Lord choose you and teach you the interpretation of dreams
and perfect His favor on you and on the offspring of Jacob,
as He perfected it on your fathers, Abraham and Isaac before!
Indeed, your Lord is All-Knowing, All-Wise.
The Qur'an, Joseph, Verses 5-6

Even though Joseph did not tell his brothers about his dream, they were extremely jealous of him and hatched a wicked plot. With seeming innocence, they asked their father's permission to take Joseph out to play. Jacob was nervous about letting Joseph go, but at the same time wished to see his sons grow close and love each other. With reluctance, he agreed.

Once out in the desert, the insincere smiles on Joseph's brothers' faces turned to vicious scowls. They discussed murdering him, but one brother urged throwing him in a well instead. That way, they would not be guilty for killing him with their own hands. The brothers agreed and flung Joseph down into the well.

Deep in the well, Joseph prayed to God to save him. This, of course, was the Lord's plan as He had an important mission for Joseph to fulfill. Shortly thereafter, a caravan on its way to Egypt stopped at the well in search of water. When they pulled their bucket out of the well, Joseph was hanging onto it! "What a handsome and well-mannered boy!" they said. "Let's take him with us to Egypt!"

Meanwhile, the brothers had returned home and reported to their father that Joseph had been eaten by a wolf. As proof, they gave Jacob his shirt covered with animal blood. This broke Jacob's heart, but he knew that somewhere somehow Joseph was alive. He prayed to God to protect and bless Joseph.

In Egypt, Joseph was adopted by a rich and powerful man called Al-Aziz, and his wife, Zulaikha. Many happy years passed. However, as Joseph matured, Zulaikha fell increasingly in love with him and tried to seduce him. Joseph rejected her advances as he did not want to engage in a sinful relationship or betray Al-Aziz, who had raised him with kindness and generosity. One day, she tried to trap Joseph and ripped the back of his shirt as he ran away. While it was clear that Zulaikha was to blame, Al-Aziz banished Joseph to prison to save the family honor.

While in prison, God gave Joseph the ability to interpret dreams, and he became known for this gift among the inmates. On one occasion, two imprisoned royal servants asked for his advice. One had dreamt that he saw himself in a vineyard plucking grapes and pressing them into wine. The other had dreamt that he was holding a basket of bread on his head, when a bird came and ate it on his head. Joseph told the first man that he would be freed from the prison to serve the king, but warned the second man that he would soon die. Shortly thereafter, the first was released and the second executed.

Years passed and Joseph remained in prison, until one day the king called for him. He was haunted by a mysterious reoccurring dream and was told by his servant that Joseph could interpret it for him. In the dream, seven fat cows were devoured by seven skinny cows; and there were seven green ears of corn and seven that were shriveled and dry. Joseph interpreted that Egypt would suffer famine, and advised the King to be ready to save his people from great suffering. He said:

What you cultivate during the next seven years,
when the time of harvest comes, leave the grains in their spikes,

except for what you eat. After that, seven years of drought will come,
which will consume most of what you stored for them. After that, a year will
come that brings relief for the people and they will, once again, press juice
The Qur'an, Chapter 2, Joseph, Verses 47-49

What Joseph prophesied came true and Egypt survived the great famine. As a result, the King said:

Bring him to me, so I can hire him to work for me."
When he talked with him, he said, "Today, you have a prominent
position with us." He (Joseph) said, "Make me the treasurer, for I am
experienced in this area and knowledgeable."
We thus established Joseph on earth, ruling as he wished.
We shower our mercy upon whomever we will, and we never fail
to recompense the righteous. Additionally, the reward in the Hereafter
is even better for those who believe and lead a righteous life."
The Qur'an, Chapter 12, Joseph, Verses 54-57

News of Egypt's prosperity spread far and wide; and people traveled from every direction to request wheat. Even Joseph's brothers came from the land of Canaan. They did not recognize him in their appeal for assistance and he gave them wheat for free. His brothers were thrilled but puzzled by his kindness.

Later, when they returned for more, they recognized Joseph. Instead of punishing them, he forgave them and they were sorry for what they had done. They went back to Canaan and returned with Joseph's parents for a joyous reunion with their long lost son. Jacob had become blind, but then God restored his vision. His beautiful son Joseph was indeed a sight to behold.

Joseph and his family settled in Egypt and were called the Israelites. While they grew in number and power, they remained isolated and were considered foreigners due to their worship of the One True God.

Yoush (Shu'ayb)

Shu'ayb was a descendant of the Prophet Abraham from the Midian tribe of the northeastern Sinai Peninsula. The Midian Arabs wandered between the rich and fertile lands of Palestine, Jordan and Egypt to tend to their livestock and bountiful crops. Aqaba was their capitol at the mouth of the Red Sea.

Like the people of Noah, Heber, Shaloh and Lot, the Midians failed to obey the teachings of the Prophets. Many were merchants and traders who placed their love of money above their love of God. They would lie, cheat and steal; and were known for giving short measures and weights to their customers. Moreover, they used their abundance of wealth to corrupt society and promote immorality. God Almighty, in His mercy, sent Shu'ayb as yet another guide to mankind.

To the Midian people we sent Shu'ayb, one of their own brethren:
He said: Oh my people, worship God! You have no other god but Him. Now
there has come to you a clear sign from your Lord! Give just measure and
weight, and do not withhold from the people the things that are their due.
And do no mischief on the earth after it has been set in order.
That will be best for you, if you have faith.
The Qur'an, Chapter 7, The Heights, Verse 85

Shu'ayb was an eloquent and powerful orator, who spoke clearly and convincingly. He constantly admonished the Midians to enjoin good and forbid evil. Nonetheless, they turned a deaf ear and ridiculed him ceaselessly. A group of tribal leaders threatened to expel him from the region and said:

The chiefs of those who were arrogant among his people said, "In the Name of God, the Most Gracious, the Most MercifulWe will certainly drive you out, Oh Shu'ayb! And those who have believed you from our town, unless you all return to our religion!"He said, "Even though we hate it? We will invent a lie against God if we return to your religion, after God has rescued us from it? It is not up to us to return unless God, our Lord, wills it. Our Lord comprehends all things in His knowledge. In God do we put our trust. Our Lord! Judge between us and our people in truth, for You are the best of judges!
The Qur'an, Chapter 7, The Heights, Verses 88-99

He reminded them of the dreadful calamities that had befallen previous nations and said:

Oh my people! Don't let this anger with mecause you to suffer the fate that befell the people of Noah,and the people of Heber, and the people of Shaloh,and the people of Lot are not far from you!
The Qur'an, Chapter 11, Heber, Verse 89

The people of Midian did not heed his words and, sure enough, a day of overshadowing gloom struck. A volcanic eruption accompanied by a shower of ashes and cinders drove them into their homes, where an earthquake finished them off.

So the earthquake seized them and they lay (dead) in their homes.
The Qur'an, Chapter 7, The Heights, Verse 91

Prophet Shu'ayb and his followers were spared and they departed to Yemen to live in peace.

Moses (Musa)

More than 3,000 years ago in the land of Egypt, Prophet Joseph and his family settled. Ancestors of the Prophet Abraham, they worshipped the One True God and were called Israelites. At that time, Egypt was polytheistic and a great number of its people worshipped false gods and goddesses. For this reason, the Israelites isolated themselves and turned to their Lord for salvation.

For 400 years, the Israelites lived peacefully in Egypt, until Ramses II became the Pharaoh. He was an arrogant tyrant who believed he was divine. Under his reign, the Children of Israel were forced into slavery and beaten. Since they rejected the Pharaoh, they were treated as outcasts and often denied basic human needs.

Though persecuted, the Israelite community continued to grow and the Pharaoh became concerned that they would take over Egypt. Thus, he devised a plan to commit genocide and ordered his minions to dispatch throughout Egypt and systematically murder each and every Israelite baby boy.

Surely Pharaoh exalted himself in the land and divided its people into parties, oppressing one party from among them by killing their sons and sparing their women. Surely he was one of the mischief-makers.
The Qur'an, Chapter 28, The Narration, Verse 4

When the people of Egypt learned of these orders, they were horrified. However, out of fear, they complied with the Pharaoh's orders. All Israelite baby boys were killed and whenever soldiers received reports that a new male infant was born, they would yank him out of his mother's arms, stab him, or throw him into the Nile River. Many innocent babies were murdered and their mothers shed tears of grief long and deep as the Nile.

At that time, a pure and devout Israelite woman named Jochebedgave birth to a beautiful and special baby boy named Moses. She knew that the Pharaoh's soldiers would soon be after him, so she pleaded with God Almighty to save him and He revealed to her the following:

Suckle him and when you fear for him, cast him into the river
and do not fear nor grieve. Surely, We will restore him to you
and make him one of the Messengers.
The Qur'an, Chapter 28, The Narration, Verse 7

And so, when Moses was a few months old, his mother wrapped him in a blanket, put him in a basket, placed it in the Nile and set him adrift. Her heart pounded as she watched her beloved baby float slowly down the river.

Eventually, the basket landed on shore. Baby Moses was found and taken to the house of the Pharaoh, while Moses' sister followed from a distance. Asiya, the Pharaoh's wife, fell in love with him and convinced her husband to keep him so that they could raise him as their son.

Suddenly, Moses started to cry in hunger and Asiya called for a nursemaid. His sister stepped forward stating that she knew where a nursemaid could be found. His mother was summoned and she gave him her breast milk, which he drank to his heart's content. Asiya then asked Jochebed to live with them as his nursemaid. God Almighty states of this miracle:

*So We restored him to his mother that her eyes might be refreshed
and that she might not grieve and that she might know
that the promise of God is true, but most of them do not know*
The Qur'an, Chapter 28, The Narration, Verse 13

So, unknown to the Pharaoh, the Prophet Moses was raised a prince under his own roof. As Moses grew, he witnessed people worshipping the Pharaoh instead of God and detested their indecent way of life. He also abhorred the cruel manner in which the Israelites were treated, since they refused to worship the Pharaoh. Although he led a luxurious life, Moses knew deep within his heart that God wanted him to change things.

Years passed and one day, when Moses was a young man, he saw an Israelite fighting one of the Pharaoh's men, who was about to kill him. Moses came to his rescue and a fight broke out in which the Egyptian was accidentally killed.

*...And he found the two men fighting, one of his party (religion) and the other
of his foes. The man of his party asked him for help against his foe,
so Moses struck him with his fist and killed him.
He said: "This is of Satan's doing. Surely, he is an open enemy leading
astray." He said: "My Lord! Indeed I have wronged myself, so forgive me."
Then He forgave him. Indeed, He is the Oft-Forgiving, the Most Merciful.*
The Qur'an, Chapter 28, The Narration, Verses 15-16

The news of the murder spread throughout Egypt and Moses was warned that Pharaoh was plotting with his court officials to kill him. He was advised to flee for his life out of Egypt. In the middle of the night, while everyone was asleep, he packed his bags and left the Pharaoh's home.

For several days and nights he traveled, asking for God's help and guidance. Finally, he arrived at Midian on the Gulf of Aqaba, where he took rest in the shade by a well. In the distance, he saw two maidens with sheep in need of help. He approached them and offered to water their flock, as they were too shy to draw near the well with so many men around.

Later, one of the maidens returned to Moses with an invitation from her father (Prophet Shu'ayb) to join the family for a meal. She said her father was grateful for the noble gesture and wished to thank him. Later, upon learning of Moses' circumstances and witnessing his fine character, the father invited Moses to stay. He gladly accepted and passed many pleasant days in Midian. Then, one day the father said:

> *I intend to marry one of these two daughters of mine to you*
> *on the condition that you should serve me for eight years,*
> *but if you complete ten years, it will be of your own free will,*
> *but I don't intend to place you under difficulty.*
> *If God wills, you will find me one of good."*
> *He (Moses) said: "That (is settled) between me and you:*
> *whichever of the two terms I fulfill, there shall be no injustice to me*
> *and God is trustee of what we say."*
> The Qur'an, Chapter 28, The Narration, Verses 27-28

Some eight years passed and Moses was happy in the company of his new family. He and his father-in-law spent hours talking about the nature of the universe and man's purpose as God's creation. Still, while he loved Midian, he had a burning desire to return to his people. With his father-in-law's blessings, he and his family set forth for Egypt.

One day, while crossing the Sinai Desert, Moses reached the mountain of Tur. There, he perceived a brilliant light in the distance and he approached it out of curiosity and to warm himself. Suddenly, he heard a voice from the right side of the valley. It thundered:

Verily, I am your Lord, so take off your shoes,
because you are in the Sacred Valley, Tuwa.
And I have chosen you, so listen to that which will be revealed.
Verily, I am God! None has the right to be worshiped but I,
so worship Me and perform prayers for My remembrance.
The Qur'an, Chapter 20, Ta-Ha, Verses 11-12

Moses, now clearly chosen to fulfill his destiny as a Prophet of God, was scared and confused. He fixated on the fire before him, which was not mere burning flames but a manifestation of the glory of God.

The Lord then engaged Moses in the ultimate miracle: He, The Almighty, spoke to him! God commanded him to throw the staff in his hand onto the ground. When he obeyed, the stick turned into a wiggling snake, which he thought was going to bite him. God directed him to pick it up. When he touched the snake, it turned once again into a stick. Soon afterwards, God ordered Moses to place his hand under his armpit. When he removed his hand, it radiated an incandescent light. Moses returned his hand to his armpit and pulled it out it out again. He found that God had restored it to its original form. With these miracles, Moses was whole-heartedly convinced of his Lord's existence and power. Moreover, he submitted himself fully to Him with fear, awe, humility and love.

God commanded Moses to go to Egypt to save the Israelites from the Pharaoh and to teach the Egyptians about the One True God and His Message. Since Moses sometimes stuttered when he spoke, He allowed him to take his brother Aaron, who was a strong and convincing speaker. Once in Egypt, Moses and Aaron went to the Pharaoh, but the king and his people were not convinced. Rather, they were annoyed by the Prophets and ridiculed them. Moses and Aaron did not give up and kept spreading the truth.

One day, Moses went to Pharaoh and asked for the opportunity to prove God's existence. When he mockingly agreed, Moses threw his staff on the ground and it transformed into a large terrifying snake. Then, to everyone's amazement, he calmly picked it up and it became a stick again. Moses then put his hand under his armpit and withdrew it shining brilliantly white and luminous.

The Pharaoh's advisors claimed that Moses was a master magician. This challenged the King of Egypt, who feared that his subjects would be wooed by Moses' advanced sorcery, forsake him and commit treason. He declared a competition pitting Moses against the best illusionists in the land. In front of thousands of spectators, the royal magicians cast their sticks, which deceptively wiggled and slithered like snakes fooling people from a distance. Then, when Moses threw his stick, God turned it into a hungry serpent and the massive stealthy snake effortlessly devoured the magicians' moving sticks. At that point, all of the magicians and most of the spectators recognized that they had witnessed a miracle of the One True God to Whom this oracle named Moses professed his devotion. The magicians threw themselves down on the ground and prostrated their foreheads in submission asking God The Almighty for mercy and forgiveness.

Pharaoh was humiliated and his power diminished. Outraged, he threatened his magicians, saying:

I shall certainly cut off your hands and your feet on opposite sides,
then I will crucify you altogether.
The Qur'an, Chapter 7, The Heights, Verses 124

He then ordered his soldiers to persecute the Israelites. Meanwhile, God directed Moses to lead his people out of Egypt. In a secret night migration, they moved quickly knowing that Pharaoh's soldiers would be on their heels in the morning.

Sure enough, upon reaching the Red Sea, the Israelites heard the thunderous sound of horses approaching. They were frightened and trapped between the oncoming soldiers and the sea. Then God spoke to the Prophet again, saying:

Strike the sea with your stick
and it parted and each part become like a large mountain.
Then We brought near the others (Pharaoh's forces) to that place;
And We saved Moses and all those with him.
Then we drowned the others.
Indeed, in this is a sign, yet most are not believers.
And verily, your Lord, He is truly The Almighty, The Most Merciful.
The Qur'an, Chapter 26, The Poets, Verse 63-68

As the Red Sea waters crashed down on Pharaoh's minions while the Israelites crossed to safety, he realized that he had been wrong about Moses and cried out to God:

Now I believe that no god exists except God
in whom the Children of Israel believe,
and I am one of those who submit to God's Will
The Qur'an, Jonah, Verse 90

The Lord rejected Pharaoh's desperate last-minute testimony of faith and he perished. His mummy was discovered in the ancient city of Thebes in 1898 and today can be viewed at the Egyptian Museum in Cairo. Describing Pharaoh's death, the Qur'an says:

This day We will save your body,
so that you will become a Sign for your predecessors.
And verily, many among mankind are heedless of Our Signs.
The Qur'an, Jonah, Verse 92

Now, the Israelites were free to worship God and live their lives in accordance with the teachings of Moses. Before carrying on to the promised land of Canaan to serve as an example for all mankind to follow, God instructed them to wander in the Sinai Desert to contemplate the magnitude of this responsibility. During this time, He shielded them from the sun by making clouds follow them wherever they went. In the parched desert terrain, He created a libation called manna, which fell as beads of dew from the sky. For meat he sent quails, which they could easily catch.

At one point, they had gone days without water and became parched with thirst. God told Moses to strike a large rock with his staff. When he did, water gushed forth from 12 different places. The nation of Israel had 12 tribes and each had its own fountain of cool clear water. Still many of them did not believe in God or appreciate the miracles He had bestowed upon them.

One day, Moses retreated up Mount Sinai to commune with his Lord, Who revealed the secrets of creation and the structure of religion. The Prophet wrote these Commandments on Tablets. In his absence, some of the Israelites constructed a statue of a golden calf, which he discovered them worshipping upon his return. Upon witnessing this disobedience, he threw down the Tablets and became extremely angry. He lamented that his people had forsaken their Lord, in spite of the multitudinous miracles they had witnessed. He and his followersthen punishedthose who had betrayed God and attempted to thwart their divine mission.

Keenly aware of God's power contrasted with the weak faith of some of his followers, Moses took the best 70 of his men to a mountain and called:

"My Lord! Show me Yourself so that I may look upon You."
He said, "You cannot bear to see Me but look at the mountain.
If it remains firm in its place, then you will see Me."
When his Lord manifested His glory to the mountain,
He made it crumble and Moses fell down unconscious.
When he recovered, he said, "Glory be to You. I turn to You in repentance and
I am the first of believers."
The Qur'an, Chapter 7, The Heights, Verse 143

The men cried to Moses to ask God to forgive them. God commanded that the Israelites sacrifice a cow. They told Moses to ask God what kind of cow.

Then they wanted to know what color it had to be. They kept on asking Moses more and more details about the cow instead of obeying their Lord.

After the Israelites had remained in the desert for some time, God told Moses to settle in an honorable dwelling place between Egypt and Syria. The Prophet sent 12 men representing the 12 Israelite tribes descending from Prophet Jacob to scout out the land. They returned with the news that it was green, fertile and had plenty of water. The land, however, was controlled by Philistine giants with strong armies and most of the Israelites were afraid to venture forth. Moses told them, "Put your trust in God, if you are true believers," but they refused. As a result, the Children of Israel wandered in the desert for another 40 years, until they mustered up the courage to enter the Promised Land.

By the time the Israelites entered the Holy Land, Moses had passed away and returned to his Lord. The Prophet died at the age of 120 on top of a mountain overlooking the Jordan Valley. In his heart, he had every intention to reach the Promised Land. However, it was God's plan that he return unto Him without completing that journey. The Children of Israel settled in the Promised Land, but continued to breech their Lord's Commandments. Thereby, they earned His wrath and He sent many more Prophets to convey His Message.

The Qur'an mentions Moses more frequently than any other Prophet, may God's peace and blessings be upon them all, and he is often referred to by the title: "He who spoke with God."

And mention in the Book (the Qur'an) Moses.
Verily, he was chosen and he was a Messenger, a Prophet.
And we called him from the right side of the Mount

and made him draw near to Us to talk.
The Qur'an, Chapter 19, Mary, Verses 51-52

As for Asiya, who adopted Moses, she will be among the first women to enter Paradise on the Day of Resurrection as she recognized the truth of Moses' Message and submitted to the One True God. This was despite the fact that she was the wife of Pharaoh – the man who claimed to be God Himself, who persecuted her terribly for challenging and disobeying him. Asiya chose the Hereafter and nearness to God above all of the wealth and power of this world.

God sets forth an example for those who believe —
the wife of Pharaoh who said: "My Lord! Build for me a home with You in
Paradise, and save me from Pharaoh and his work,
and save me from the nation of wrong-doers."
The Qur'an, Chapter 66, The Prohibition, Verse 11

Aaron (Harun)

The Prophet Aaron was the older brother of Moses, who relied on him to help with the God-given mission of saving the Israelites from the Egyptian Pharaoh. The Israelites were the inheritors of the teachings of the Prophets, and the Pharaoh demanded that they commit the greatest sin by worshipping him instead of God!

Indeed, We bestowed Our favor on Moses and Aaron,
and we delivered them and their people from great disaster,
and We helped them, so they overcame their troubles,
and We gave them the Book (the Torah) which helps make things clear,
and We guided them to the Straight Path.
And We left this blessing for future generations.
Peace and salutation to Moses and Aaron!
The Qur'an, Chapter 37, Those Arranged in Ranks, Verses 114-120

Moses had a speech impediment, so he asked God to allow Aaron, who was a gifted speaker, to assist him.

And my brother, Aaron, he is more eloquent of tongue than I.
Therefore, send him with me as a helper, verifying me.
Surely, I fear that they would reject me." He (God) said: "We will certainly
strengthen your arm through your brother, and invest you both with authority,
so they will not be able to touch you. With Our Sign you will triumph -- you
two as well as those who follow you.
The Qur'an, Chapter 28, The Narration, Verses 34-35

After Moses and Aaron saved the Israelites from the Pharaoh's forces, which God swallowed up in the Red Sea, they retreated to the Sinai to establish their own community. Often Moses would retreat to Mount Sinai, to contemplate God's greatness and his divine mission. One day, he descended from the mountain with tablets conveying God's Commandments and found his people worshipping an idol in the shape of a golden calf. Moses was furious and blamed Aaron.

And when Moses returned to his people, wrathful (and) in violent grief,
he said, Evil is what you have done after me. Did you turn away from the
bidding of your Lord?" And he threw down the tablets and seized his brother
by the head, dragging him towards him. He said, "Son of my mother! Surely
the people reckoned me weak and have almost killed me. Therefore, do not let
the enemies rejoice over me and
do not include me among the unjust people."
The Qur'an,Chapter 7, The Heights, Verse 150

Aaron replied: Oh, son of my mother!
Seize (me) not by my beard nor by (the hair of) my head!
Truly I feared you would say, 'You have caused a division among the children
of Israel, and you did not respect my word!'"
The Qur'an,Chapter20, Ta Ha, Verse 94

Thus, Aaron professed his innocence and contempt for the idol-worshippers and their deeds. He joined with Moses and their followers to slay those who had conspired against the divine mission of the Children of Israel. Imagine, after all the miracles they had witnessed and guidance and protection they had received, some chose to defy the Lord!

David (Dawood)

Once upon a time, in the city of Bethlehem, there lived the Prophet David, who was a descendant of the Prophet Jacob. David was the youngest of eight brothers, very handsome, musically gifted, and had the face of an angel. He was also a fearless young shepherd known to have killed a lion and bear. David was a pious child, who believed in God and tried to please Him.

At that time, Saul was the King of the Israelites. He was a God-fearing man, whose people were at war with the polytheistic Philistines. Goliath was a gigantic Philistine soldier, who boasted that if any one of the Israelites overpowered him, he and his men would surrender. Meanwhile, none of Saul's men was courageous enough to accept the challenge.

Young David insisted on joining the army. King Saul gave him a helmet and armor, but the boy would not don them. He gave him a sword, but he refused to accept it. David said that his strength and protection came from God Almighty. He took his sling, chose five smooth stones from a brook, and proceeded to lead the Israelites to fight the giant. He knew that, with God's blessings and protection, it was possible to win.

When they marched forth to face Goliath and his troops, they said:
"Our Lord, fill us full of patience and make our steps firm.
Support us against the disbelievers!"
The Qur'an, Chapter 2, The Cow, Verse 250

David stepped forward to fight the giant, who cursed at him in the name of false deities. The boy replied, "I have come against you in the name of the Lord Almighty, Whom you have defied," and hurled a stone at Goliath.

It landed squarely in the center of the behemoth's forehead and he fell down dead.

They routed them with God's permission and David killed Goliath;
and God gave him the kingdom and Prophethood
and taught him that which He willed.
If God did not check one set of people by means of another,
the earth would indeed be full of mischief.
But, God possesses bounty for the Universe.

The Qur'an, Chapter 2, The Cow, Verse 251

And so, with the demise of Goliath, the Israelites chased the Philistines out of the land and won an enormous victory. After King Saul's death, David became the beloved King of Israel. Moreover, he was recognized as a Prophet of God, who delivered the Message of the Psalms to his people.

"In the Name of God, the Most Gracious, the Most Merciful
We have sent you inspiration, as We sent it to Noah and the Messengers after him. We sent inspiration to Abraham, Ishmael, Isaac, Jacob and the Tribes, to Jesus, Job, Jonah, Aaron, and Solomon, and to David we gave the Psalms."
The Qur'an, Chapter 4, The Women, Verse 163

The Book of Psalms is referred to in the Qur'an as one of God's Books revealed to five Messengers. It contains words of wisdom andprayers exalting the Lord Most High and conveys a range of human emotion and experience. This Holy Book ispreceded by the Scrolls given to Abraham and the Torah delivered unto Moses. It is followed by the Gospel of Jesus and the Qur'an as bestowed toMuhammad, may God's peace and blessings be upon them all.

Solomon (Sulayman)

As a boy, Solomon learned a great deal from his father, Prophet David; and the Lord had bestowed the finest spiritual and moral character on both father and son. Moreover, David was the King of Israel and Solomon was rich in all manners of wealth and status.

As a young boy, Solomon was not concerned with material matters or social prestige. Rather, he was preoccupied with the ethereal qualities and manifestations of life. In tone with nature, he chose birds and animals among his companions; and God taught him the language of many creatures including jinn. Also, Solomon was blessed with the gifts of wisdom, honesty and fairness, which earned him the love and loyalty of his people. At the age of 13, he assumed the throne of the Kingdom of Israel.

> *Indeed, We gave knowledge to David and Solomon,*
> *and they both said:"Praise be to God, Who has favored us*
> *above many of His believing servants."*
> *And Solomon was David's heir, and he said:*
> *"O men! We have been taught the language of birds*
> *and we have been given all things; most surely this is manifest grace."*
> The Qur'an,Chapter 27, The Ants, Verses 15 -16

Solomon knew, as do all creatures, that all goodness comes from God. He told his people to praise the Lord for their many blessings. He inculcated in his kingdom the imperative of worshipping God alone and doing good deeds.

No creature was too small for the Prophet's attention and concern. One day, he and his soldiers passed through a valley inhabited by ants and he heard an ant speaking.

And there were gathered before Solomon his groups of jinn and men and
birds, and they all were set in battle order.
Until, when they reached the Valley of the Ants, an ant exclaimed:
"Oh ants! Enter your houses or else Solomon and his armies
will crush you without realizing it."
So Solomon smiled, amused at her speech; and he said:
"O my Lord! Order me to be grateful for Your favors,
which You have bestowed on me and on my parents,
and that I may work the righteousness that will please You:
And admit me, by Your Grace, to the ranks of Your righteous servants."
The Qur'an,Chapter 27, The Ants, Verses 17-19

He then ordered his soldiers to halt until all the ants had crawled to safety.

One day, Solomon assembled all the birds around him, but as he scanned the flocks, he noticed that the Hoopoe bird was not there. He waited for some time before the Hoopoe suddenly flew in and alighted by his side. "I have come from a far-away city called Sheba," the Hoopoe said. "The people there are very rich and have a queen who sits on a magnificent throne. These people worship the sun and believe they are correct to treat the sun as God. But they are wrong, are they not? God is the only One Whom all creatures should worship."

Solomon then wrote a letter to the Queen of Sheba and sent the Hoopoe to deliver it. When the queen received it, she called together the wise men of the city to show them the letter. In it, Solomon implored the people of Sheba to believe in God and worship only Him. She asked her advisers for counsel.

Some of the wise men appealed to the powerful queen to declare war against Solomon. She rejected this idea outright stating that war could cause destruction to Sheba, while turning their men into cruel fighters. "Rather than declare war," she said, "I will send Solomon a present instead."

When the queen dispatched her messengers to Solomon, they presented her gift and were astonished by his angry response. "Why do you bring me riches instead of listening to my advice?" he admonished. "What God has given me is much better than all these riches. Return to your queen and take her presents with you!"

When she heard that Solomon had refused her fine gifts, the Queen of Sheba was astonished. So, she decided to pay a visit to King Solomon herself. She called together her closest advisers and made preparations for the journey. Meanwhile, he received her response to meet him and asked one of the advisors to bring him to her mansion before her arrival. One of the jinn said:

"In the Name of God, the Most Gracious, the Most Merciful I can bring it to you in the twinkling of an eye." When Solomon saw it settled in front of him, he said, "This is a blessing from my Lord, whereby He tests me, to show whether I am grateful or ungrateful. Whoever is grateful is grateful for his own good, and if one turns ungrateful, then my Lord is Free of All Needs, Most Honorable."He said, "Remodel her mansion for her. Let us see if she will be guided, or continue with the misguided.

"In the Name of God, the Most Gracious, the Most Merciful
"When she arrived, she was asked, "Does your mansion look like this?"
She said, "It seems that this is it." Solomon said, "We knew beforehand what
she was going to do, and we were already submitters."
She had been diverted by worshipping idols instead of God.
She belonged to disbelieving people. She was told, "Go inside the palace."
When she saw its interior, she thought it was a pool of water,
and she (pulled up her dress,) exposing her legs.
He said, "This interior is now paved with crystal."
She said, "My Lord, I have wronged my soul.
I now submit with Solomon to God, Lord of the universe."
The Qur'an, Chapter 27, The Ants, Verses 40-44

Prophet Solomon then married the queen, whose name was Bilqees. Thereafter, she returned to her land, where he visited her frequently. The people of Sheba listened to them expound upon the magnificent attributes of God and embraced monotheism. From that point on, the people of the region, now the countries of Ethiopia, Eritrea, Djibouti, Somalia and Yemen, have practiced monotheism and are known for their piety.

Later, as an old man, Solomon stood leaning on his staff viewing the construction of the Holy Temple and expansion and development of the city of Jerusalem.

And before Solomon were marshalled his hosts –
of jinn, and men, and birds,
and they were all marching in rows.
The Qur'an, Chapter 27, The Ants, Verse 17

A man approached him. Surprised, he asked, "Who are you and who gave you permission to enter the palace?" The visitor replied, "I have come with the permission of God, the Owner of the Universe. I am the Angel of Death and God has sent me to take your life away." Solomon responded, "Then discharge your duty." And, he began to pray.

Then, as he leaned upon his staff, his soul left him. His body remained standing upright, while the jinn and men and birds continued building the kingdom. They carried on industriously for some time under his apparent view. Finally, the staff upon which he was leaning crumbled and his body fell to the ground.

"In the Name of God, the Most Gracious, the Most Merciful
Then when We decreed death for him,
nothing informed them of his death except a little worm of the earth,
which kept gnawing away at his stick.
So when he fell down, the jinn saw clearly that if they had known the unseen,
they would not have stayed in the humiliating torment.
The Qur'an, Chapter 34, Sheba, Verse 14

Job (Ayoub)

The Prophet Job was a descendant of Abraham and a great tradition of Prophets. As God says in the Holy Book:

> *"In the Name of God, the Most Gracious, the Most Merciful*
> *That was Our proof, which We gave Abraham against his people.*
> *We raise whom We will in degrees.*
> *Certainly your Lord is All-Wise, All-Knowing.*
> *And We bestowed upon him Isaac and Jacob,*
> *each of them We guided and before him,*
> *David, Solomon, Job, Joseph, Moses and Aaron.*
> *Thus do We reward the good doers.*
> The Qur'an, The Cattle, Verses 83-84

One day, a group of angels was discussing God's creatures besides themselves. They came upon the topic that humans are often quite arrogant. Then one said, "The best creature on earth today is Job, a man of noble character who displays great patience and always remembers his generous Lord. He is a great example to follow for those who wish to worship God. That's why God has blessed him with a long life, wealth and plenty of servants; and he shares his fortune by helping the needy. He feeds and clothes the poor and buys slaves to set them free. He is so kind and gentle, that he makes those who receive his charity feel as if they are doing him a favor!"

Satan overheard this and was filled with contempt. He plotted and schemed how he could destroy Job's esteemed status by seducing him to become a sinner. In vain, he tried to distract Job from his prayers by whispering temptations in his ear. Nonetheless, Job was steadfast and

71

would not let evil thoughts lure him. This disturbed Satan and he reviled Job even more.

Satan complained that Job was insincere in his constant praise of the Lord. Rather, he argued that Job was a phony who pretended to be good so that God would lavish him in riches. "If You remove his wealth," he told the Lord, "then You will find that his tongue will no longer mention Your Name and he will stop praying," said Satan.

God told Satan that Job was one of His most sincere devotees and that he did not revere Him because of the favors. Nonetheless, to prove him wrong, He permitted the devil to do whatever he and his demons wished with Job's wealth.

Satan was enraptured as he assembled his helpers fiendishly instructing them to destroy all of Job's servants, cattle and farms. Rubbing his hands in glee, he appeared before Job disguised as a wise old man and said: "All your wealth is lost and some people say that it is because you gave too much charity and that you are wasting your time with your continuous prayers to God. Others say that God has punished you in order to please your enemies. If God had the capacity to prevent harm, then He would have protected your wealth." True to his belief, Job replied: "What God has taken away from me belongs to Him. I was only its trustee for awhile. He gives to whom He wills and withholds from whom He wills." With these words, Job prostrated to his Lord in prayer.

When Satan saw this, he felt frustrated and lamented to God: "I have stripped Job of all his possessions, but he still remains grateful to You. However, he is only hiding his disappointment. What he cares most about is his offspring. You will see how Job rejects You, if you try him with his children." So, God granted Satan permission to test Job through his sons and daughters, but warned that it would not reduce Job' faith in His Lord or his patience.

Again, Satan gathered his helpers and set about his evil deeds. He shook the foundation of the house in which Job's children were living and sent the building crashing down killing them all. Then, he went to Job disguised as a man who had come to sympathize with him. In a comforting tone he said to Job, "The circumstances under which your children died were sad. Surely, your Lord is not rewarding you properly for all your prayers."

Having said this, Satan confidently waited for Job to finally reject God, but again the Prophet disappointed him by replying, "God sometimes gives and sometimes takes. He is sometimes pleased and sometimes displeased with our deeds. Whether a thing is beneficial or harmful to me, I will remain firm in my belief and thankful to my Creator." Then, Job prostrated to his Lord in prayer.

At this, Satan was infuriated and declared, "Oh my Lord, Job's wealth is gone, his children are dead, but he is still healthy in body! As long as he enjoys good health, he will continue to worship You in the hope of regaining his wealth and producing more children! Grant me authority over his body so that I may weaken it. He will surely neglect worshipping You and will thus become disobedient!"

God wanted to teach Satan the lesson that Job was His devoted servant, so He granted his third request. However, he placed upon it a condition and said, "I give you authority over his body, but not over his soul, intellect or heart, for in these places reside the knowledge of Me and My religion."

Armed with renewed conviction and empowerment, Satan took revenge on Job's body and afflicted it with a multitude of disease, until he was reduced to skin and bones and suffering severe pain. In spite of all of his agony, however, Job remained steadfast in his faith and patiently bore all of his hardships without complaining. He turned to no one for help, but asked God alone for His mercy.

Meanwhile, all of his close relatives and friends deserted him. Only his loving and loyal wife stood by his side. In his time of need, she showered her kindness on him and cared for his ailments. She remained his sole companion through many years of suffering.

With this, Satan became desperate. He consulted his helpers, but they could not advise him. They asked, "How is it that your deception cannot work against Job, yet you were successful in leading Adam, the father of man, out of Paradise?"

Satan then had a plan. He went to Job's wife in the form of a man. "Where is your husband?" he asked. She pointed to an almost lifeless form crumpled on the bed and said, "There he is, suspended between life and death." Satan reminded her of the days when Job was healthy, wealthy and had children. Suddenly, the painful memory of years of hardship overcame her and she burst into tears. She complained to Job, "How long are you going to bear this torture from our Lord? Are we to remain without wealth, children or friends forever? Why don't you ask God to remove this suffering?"

Job sighed and in a soft voice replied, "Satan must have whispered to you and made you dissatisfied. Tell me how long did I enjoy good health and riches?" She replied, "80 years." Then Job asked, "How long have I been suffering like this?" She said, "Seven years." He then told her, "In that case, I am ashamed to call on my Lord to remove the hardship, because my years of abundance are more than my years of hardship. It seems your faith has weakened and you are dissatisfied with what God has given us. If I ever regain health, I swear I will punish you with a hundred strokes! From this day onward, I forbid myself to eat or drink anything by your hand. Leave me alone and let my Lord do with me as He pleases."

Sobbing bitterly and with a heavy heart, Job's wife had no choice but to leave and seek shelter elsewhere. In this helpless state, he turned to God, not to complain but to seek His mercy, and said:

Indeed, Satan has touched me with hardship and torment."
The Qur'an,Chapter 38, Saad, Verse 41

So the Most Merciful God replied:

"In the Name of God, the Most Gracious, the Most Merciful
Strike the ground with your foot. This is a spring of water
to wash in and a cool and refreshing drink."
And We gave him back his family, and along with them the like thereof
as a mercy from Us, and a reminder for those who understand.
The Qur'an,Chapter 28, Saad, Verses 42-43

Meanwhile, Job's wife could no longer bear to be parted from her husband and returned to him begging for his forgiveness. Upon entering the house, she was amazed at the sudden change. Job was healthy again! She hugged him and thanked God for His mercy.

But Job, as happy as he was, remembered that he had taken an oath to punish his wife with a hundred strokes if he regained his health. Meanwhile, he had no desire to hurt her. He knew if he did not fulfill the oath, he would be guilty of breaking a promise to God. Therefore, God, in His wisdom and mercy, came to the assistance of His faithful servant and told him:

And take in your hand a bundle of thin grass and strike therewith and do not break your oath." Truly, We found him patient. How excellent a slave! Indeed, he was often returning in repentance.
The Qur'an, Saad, Verses 44

And thus, upon his death, Job was granted entry to the everlasting Gardens of Paradise to dwell eternally in the company of his Lord.

Ezekiel (Dhul-kifl)

Immediately following Job's story in the Qur'an, God Almighty directed:

And remember Our slaves, Abraham, Isaac, and Jacob,
owners of strength and religious understanding.
Indeed, We did choose them by granting them
the remembrance of the dwelling place in the Hereafter
and they used to make the people remember it;
and they also used to invite people to obey God
and do good deeds for the Hereafter.
And they are in Our Sight, indeed, of the chosen and the best!
And remember Ishmael, Elisha and Ezekiel, all among the best.
The Qur'an, Chapter 28, Saad, Verses 45-48

Prophet Ezekiel lived approximately 2600 years ago, after the Kingdom of Israel established by Saul, David and Solomon had broken into the Kingdoms of Israel and Judah in the north and south. He received many Revelations from God and admonished widespread corruption in the lands. He chastised the people for deviating from the teachings of the Prophets and prophesied that Jerusalem and the Holy Temple would be destroyed.

Sure enough, Ezekiel's predictions were fulfilled. The tyrant King Nebuchadnezzar of Babylon conquered Israel and Judah slaughtering many innocent people. Hecaptured the city of Jerusalem and ravaged the Holy Temple. He deported masses of prominent citizens to Babylon, while thousands more fled his wrath.

While in exile, Ezekiel openly rejected Nebuchadnezzar and denounced him as an evil, illegitimate ruler who did not follow the teachings of the Prophets. As a result of his brave resistance, Ezekiel was bound, shackled and thrown in prison. For a long time, he could not speak and, in midst of his suffering, exercised great forbearance and constantly worshipped God.

And (remember) Ishmael and Enoch and Ezekiel, all men of patience.
We admitted them to Our mercy, for they were of the righteous ones."
The Qur'an, The Prophets, Verses 85-86

Finally, Ezekiel was released from prison and he continued to receive Revelations commanding the Children of Israel to reclaim the Holy Land and restore the practice of God's Law. As an oracle, he traversed hither and yon between spiritual and worldly realms and eventually died in exile. Today, his tomb can be found in the town of Al Kifl, south of Babylon, in modern-day Iraq.

Jonah (Yunus)

In what is now Iraq, near the city of Mosul, along the East Bank of the Tigris River, there lived the people of Nineveh. This ancient city was an important junction on the great Silk Road trade route between the Mediterranean Sea and the Indian Ocean. As a vibrant hub uniting East and West, wealth flowed into Nineveh and it was one of richest cities in the lands. However, the people took their wealth for granted, lived a decadent lifestyle and worshipped idols.

Eventually, God sent the Prophet Jonah to the Ninevites to teach them to worship Him and to obey His Laws. However, many refused arguing, "We and our forefathers have worshipped these gods for many years and no harm has come to us." Jonah tried to convince them of the foolishness of idolatry, but they ignored him. He warned that if they persisted, God would punish them like so many fallen nations before. In their arrogance, they replied, "Let it happen!" Jonah, in his frustration, chose to abandon his charge. He left Nineveh without God's permission.

And (remember) Jonah, when he went off in anger,
and imagined that We shall not punish him!"
The Qur'an,Chapter 21, The Prophets, Verse 87

As soon as Jonah left the city, the skies changed color and appeared on fire. The people were terrified by this sight and recalled the Prophet's warnings of destruction as was faced by the peoples of Noah, Heber, Shaloh, Lot and Shu'ayb. Was theirs to be a similar fate?

With newfound faith and clarity penetrating their hearts, they gathered on a mountain to plead to God for His forgiveness; and the surrounding mountains echoed with their cries. It was a momentous occasion filled with sincere repentance. As a result, God withdrew His wrath and showered His blessings upon them once again.

Was there any town that believed after seeing the punishment,
and its faith at that moment saved it from punishment?
(The answer is none) except the people of Jonah. When they believed,
We removed from them the torment of disgrace in the life of the present world,
and permitted them to enjoy for awhile.
The Qur'an,Chapter 10, Jonah, Verse 98

When the threat of cataclysm had lifted, the people of Nineveh prayed for the return of Jonah and his guidance.

Meanwhile, the Prophet had boarded a small ship in the company of other passengers. It sailed all day in placid waters with a steady wind moving it along at a good clip. When night came, however, the sea changed. A tempest descended threatening to break the ship asunder. Torrential waves rose high as mountains crashing upon the vessel. Water swept the deck nearly submerging its passengers.

Behind the ship, at God's command, one of the largest whales in the sea trailed the vessel. Obeying his Creator, the huge dark creature rose from the water's depths spewing geysers of seawater from its spout.

The storm continued to menace the boat and the captain called upon passengers to jettison its heavy load. They threw their baggage into the sea, but the boat continued to sink. Finally, the captain decided to throw overboard one of the passengers. He was a polytheist who thought that sacrificing a human to the gods of the wind and sea might save the ship.

At his order, they cast a lot. Jonah's name was drawn, but since they knew that he was the most honorable among them, they drew a second lot. Jonah's name was drawn again. They gave him a final chance and drew a third lot. Again, his name came up again.

Jonah realized that God had planned this calamity for him, because he had abandoned his mission in Nineveh. He stood at the edge of the ship looking into the unfathomably deep, dark and angry sea. There was no moon and the sky was pitch black. In the depths of despair, faith and destiny prevailed as he plunged down...down...down beneath the raging surface into the bowels of the ocean. He kept repeating God's name as he descended the still depths of the onyx sea.

Suddenly, Jonah landed with a gurgling whoosh and a thud. The whale had found him, taken him into his mouth, and locked him behind the bars of his ivory teeth. Then, he swallowed him into his putrid stomach, where Jonah was engulfed in the stench and ooze of bile. The great fish dove to the bottom of the sea.

Three layers of oblivion enveloped the Prophet: the darkness of the whale's stomach; the darkness of the bottom of the sea; and the darkness of night. Jonah imagined himself to be dead, but his senses were alert. Yet, a glimmer of light, hope and faith remained. He knew that he was alive and his heart and tongue moved in remembrance of God.

But he cried through the darkness saying,
"None has the right to be worshipped except You (God),
glorified and exalted are You!
Truly, I have been of the wrong-doers."
The Qur'an,Chapter 21, The Prophets, Verse 87

Jonah continued praying to God, repeating this invocation. Whales, fish, algae and all the creatures of the sea listened to the celebration of God's Name emanating from the whale's stomach. All gathered around and joined in the praise of God, each chanting in its own way and language. The whale also sang the praises of God, understanding that it had swallowed a Prophet. Although it felt anxious by this strange occurrence, it consoled itself saying, "Why should I be afraid, since God commanded me to swallow him?"

God Almighty accepted Jonah's sincere repentance and ordered the whale to swim to the farthest side of the ocean and cast him ashore. The whale obeyed and ejected Jonah onto the warm earth of a remote island.

"In the Name of God, the Most Gracious, the Most Merciful
So We answered his call and delivered him from distress;
and thus do we deliver the believers."
The Qur'an, Chapter 21, The Prophets, Verse 88

Jonah's body was blistered because of the acids inside the whale's stomach; and when the sun rose, its rays burned his raw flesh and he was the verge of screaming in pain. However, he endured the pain and continued his invocations to God.

The Almighty then caused a vine to grow over the Prophet to provide him protection. Then, He healed Jonah and forgave him. God, Who is the Most Merciful and All-Compassionate, told Jonah that had he not prayed to Him, he would have languished in the whale's stomach until the Day of Judgment.

Gradually, the Prophet Jonah regained his strength and found his way home to Nineveh. He rejoiced at finding that great change that had taken place. The entire population turned out to welcome him and rejoiced that they had turned to believe in the One True God. Together they joined in prayer giving all praise and thanks to the Lord.

And, indeed, Jonah was one of the Messengers. When he ran to the laden ship, he agreed to cast lots and he was among the losers. Then a big fish swallowed him and he had done an act worthy of blame. Had he not been of those who glorify God, he would have remained inside its belly until the Day of Resurrection. But, We cast him forth on the naked shore while he was sick and We caused a gourd plant to grow over him. And We sent him to a hundred thousand people or even more, and they believed; so We gave them enjoyment for a while."
The Qur'an, Chapter 37, Those Ranged in Ranks, Verses 139-148

Elijah (Elias)

After the death of the Prophet Solomon, Satan took over the Kingdom of Israel and it fell apart. A series of corrupt kings occupied the throne and King Ahab was the worst of them all. He and his wife, Jezebel, were heathens and, rather than worship God, they idolized statues of a false god named Baal, which were associated with Satan himself. Those who believed in the God of Abraham, Moses and David were mocked, shunned or killed. Even the neighbor of the king and queen was executed and his land appropriated, because he refused to follow their pagan rituals.

In the wake of this blasphemy and desecration of the Holy Land, God delivered Prophet Elijah, a descendant of Aaron, to reform the Children of Israel. Elijah was a great leader and servant of the Lord, who warned Ahab to give up his evil ways and return the land to the neighbor's orphan child. He reminded the people of their noble heritage and destiny inextricably linked to the worship of the One True God. He forbade them praying to Baal and attempted to lead them in prayer to the Lord.

The king ignored Elijah and threatened to kill him. In spite of this, Elijah returned to the king, whose son was deathly ill, and warned him that severe drought and famine would strike the kingdom if he did not change his ways. He told him that Baal would be powerless to prevent his son's death or the starvation of his people. The king paid no heed to Elijah's warnings and, soon after, his prophecy came true. Israel was struck by famine and many died of starvation.

Elijah prayed to the Lord to have mercy on the people, who had begun to repent and ask for His forgiveness. God decreed the draught and famine to end and rain came pouring down.

And indeed, Elijah was one of the Messengers.
When he said to his people, "Will you not fear God!
And you call upon Baal and forsake the Best of Creators,
God, your Lord and the Lord of your forefathers?"
But they denied him, so they certainly will be punished.
Except the chosen slaves of God.
And we left for him a good remembrance among the later generations.
Peace be upon Elijah!
Indeed, this is how We reward those
who do good deeds totally and only for the sake of God.
Indeed, Elijah was one of the believing slaves."
The Qur'an, Chapter 37, Those Arranged In Ranks, Verses 123-132

Soon after, Elijah mysteriously vanished into the realm and protection of God.

Elisha (Al-Yasa')

Prophet Elijah appointed Prophet Elisha to follow in his footsteps by living among the people and calling them to God. He preached powerfully throughout the land and had the distinction of prophesying through the reign of four kings of Israel.

And Zechariah and John and Jesus and Elijah,
all in the ranks of the righteous;
and Ishmael and Elisha, and Jonah and Lot;
and each of them We preferred above the nations;
and from their fathers and progeny and brethren,
We chose them and guided them to a Straight Path.
The Qur'an,Chapter 6, The Cattle, Verses 85-87

After Elisha died, dissension rose among the people and Israel returned to the rule of tyrants who did not worship, fear or love God. In fact, some of them even killed Prophets.

Zechariah (Zakariya)

Prophet Zechariah, a descendant of Prophets Jacob and Solomon, did not have any children. His wife was barren and, as they reached old age, he became very worried that God would not grant him offspring. It was his greatest wish to raise a son to lead the next generation to follow the teachings of the Prophets, a son with whom God would be very pleased.

Despite that he was frail, feeble and grey-haired, Zechariah went to the temple each day to deliver his sermons. He continued to guide those who wished to be guided to the Straight Path. He dreaded what would happen to the people of Israel were he to pass away. Would they abandon God's teachings and change the Holy Laws to suit their own whims and desires?

One day, while at the temple, he prayed in seclusion:

"Oh, my Lord! Grant me from You, a good offspring.
You are indeed the All-Hearer of calls."
The Qur'an, Chapter 3, The People of Imraan, Verse 38

Lo and behold, the angels summoned him with news of a son:

God gives you glad tidings of John, witnessing the truth of a word from God,
and noble, chaste, and a Prophet from among the righteous.
The Qur'an, Chapter 3, The People of Imraan, Verse 39

Prophet Zechariah, who was more than 90 years old, responded in disbelief:

"O my Lord! How can I have a son
when I am very old and my wife is barren?"
God said: "Thus God does what He wills."
He said: "O my Lord! Make a sign for me."
God said: "Your sign is that you shall not speak to anyone
for three days but with signals.
And remember your Lord much (by praising Him constantly),
and glorify Him in the afternoon and in the morning."
The Qur'an, Chapter 3, The People of Imraan, Verses 40-41

When Zechariah left his private place of prayer, he found that he could not speak; and for three days, he praised and worshipped God the Almighty constantly. When this period had passed, his speech was restored miraculously and he knew that he and his wife were going to have a son. When the baby was born, they named him John.

Fortified in faith by this miracle, Zechariah continued preaching the religion of God and speaking out against profane, unethical and immoral behavior. One day, the most wicked among the evil doers decided to kill him and he hid without success inside the hollow of a tree. When his enemies found him, they sawed the tree in half. The Prophet did not utter a word as his body was cut into two pieces. He put his complete trust in God and prepared to meet his Lord in the Hereafter.

Today, Zechariah's murderers are condemned to the eternal fires of Hell. In the Qur'an, God tells us:

Indeed, those who disbelieve the Signs of God and kill the Prophets
wrongfully and kill those of mankind who order just dealings
then announce to them a painful torment.

They are those whose works will be lost in this world
and in the Hereafter, and they will have no helpers.
The Qur'an,Chapter 3, The People of Imraan, Verses 21-22

John (Yahya)

The Prophet John was a stoic baby; and then he was an intensely serious child. While other children played, John was pious and worshipped God all of the time. While other kids had fun, he was studious and read the Torah. The Lord said:

"O John! Hold fast to the Scripture."
And We gave him wisdom while yet a child.
The Qur'an, Chapter 19, Mary, Verse 12

The Lord guided John to love the Hebrew Scriptures; and thus he became the most devout and knowledgeable man of his time. Moreover, He endowed him with wisdom to interpret Holy Law, justice to oversee the affairs of men, and righteous character to guide others to the Straight Path.

Prophet John, like his father Prophet Zechariah, was known for complete and utter devotion to God. Once, when Zechariah did not see his son for three days, he searched for him high and low. Eventually, he found him weeping inside a grave, which he had dug for himself. He said, "My son, I have been searching for you, and you are dwelling in this grave weeping!" John replied, "Oh father, didn't you tell me that between Paradise and Hell is only a span, and it will not be crossed except by the tears of weepers?" Zechariah responded empathetically, "Weep then, my son," and so they wept together.

John cried so much that his cheeks were stained. Many nights, he would stay up shedding tears and praising God for His blessings. In the wee hours of solitary darkness, he loved to contemplate the Lord's presence and said, "The dwellers of Paradise are sleepless out of the sweetness of God's bounty. Thus, the faithful must be sleepless because of God's love in their hearts. How far between the two luxuries," he asked. "How far between them?"

He was an utterly simple and humble man, who found great comfort in nature. He didn't care about food and would eat leaves, grass, herbs, and locusts. Sometimes, he slept in the mountains. At other times, he would sleep in holes in the ground. Animals recognized his piety and, upon seeing him, were reminded to bow their heads in submission to God. Often, John gave animals the little food he had as nourishment for his own soul.

John guided many to worship the One True God; and he led many to weep in submission to Him as well. His words of true devotion arrested their hearts and liberated their souls.

One day a conflict took place between John and Herod, then the King of Israel. Herod was in love with Salome, his brother's daughter, and planned to marry her. John protested the marriage saying that it was against the Law of the Torah for a man to marry his niece. He said that such a marriage would earn the wrath of God. Upon hearing this, Salome became outraged and, as a condition of marriage, demanded that Herod kill John. He obliged her wish and brought her the Prophet's head.

While Herod and Salome were sinfully happy for a short time, God the Almighty avenged the death of His beloved Prophet. The Master of the Heavens and the Earth punished them by sending armies to invade and destroy their kingdom.

As for the Prophet John, he is in eternal bliss. His abode is in the Kingdom of Heaven near His Lord.

And peace be upon him (John),
the day he was born, the day he dies,
and the day he will be raised up to life (again)!
The Qur'an,Chapter 19, Mary, Verse 15

Jesus-the son of Mary ('IssaIbn Maryam)

Mary was one of the purest, most pious maidens who ever lived. Descendant of the Prophet David and daughter of Imraan, she lived during terrible times when Rome occupied the Holy Land and idol worship was rampant. God Almighty continued sending Prophets, but the majority of the people did not take heed.

We made a covenant with the tribe of Israel and sent Messengers to them. Each time a Messenger came to them with something their lower selves did not desire, they denied some and they murdered others.
The Qur'an,Chapter 5, The Table, Verse 70

Meanwhile, the Children of Israel anticipated the coming of a new Prophet heralded as the Messiah, who would be their savior. Unknown to Mary, God had chosen her for the most noble of duties. She would give birth to this Messenger. God said:

His name is the Messiah, Jesus, Son of Mary, of high esteem in this world and the Hereafter, and one of those brought near. He will speak to people in the cradle and in manhood, and will be one of the believers.
The Qur'an,Chapter 3, The People of Imraan, Verses 45-46

For Mary, this was strange and incredible news. She asked the Lord how it was possible that she could bear a child, when she was unmarried and no man had touched her. God Almighty said:

Even so, God creates what He wills.
When He has decreed a plan, He says to it: "Be!" - and it is.
And He will teach him the Book and the Wisdom

and the Torah and the Gospel.
The Qur'an,Chapter 3, The People of Imraan, Verses 47-48

And so, the Lord created Prophet Jesus in a most unique way. He was born without a father. Similarly, Prophet Adam and his wife Eve were born without either a father or mother.

The likeness of Jesus before God is as that of Adam.
He created him of dust, then said to him: "Be!" and he was.
The Qur'an,Chapter 3, The People of Imraan, Verse 59

Indeed, the life of Jesus, from his conception to his ascension to heaven, was full of miracles. After Mary gave birth, she brought baby Jesus to her people, who accused her of having a baby out of wedlock. They dishonored and shunned her, declaring that she was unchaste. The Angel Gabriel had warned her not to respond to these allegations. Rather, he told her to fast and remain silent. In response to their scorn, she was told to point to baby Jesus.

They said, "How can we talk to one who is a child in the cradle?"
He said: "Verily! I am a slave of God.
He has given me the Revelation and made me a Prophet;
and He has made me blessed wherever I am;
and enjoined on me prayer and giving charity as long as I live.
He has made me kind to my mother, and not overbearing or miserable.
So peace be upon me the day I was born, the day I die,
and the day I shall be raised up again!"
The Qur'an,Chapter 19, Mary, Verses 29-33

When Jesus had grown into a man, he approached his people saying:

I have come to you with a sign from your Lord, that I design for you out of clay
a figure like that of a bird, and breathe into it,
and it becomes a bird by God's leave;
and I heal him who was born blind, and the leper,
and I bring the dead to life by God's leave;
and I inform you of what you eat and store in your houses.
Surely, in that is a sign for you if you are believers.
And, I have come confirming the Torah before me,
and to make lawful some of that which was forbidden unto you.
I come to you with a sign from your Lord,
so keep your duty to God and obey me.
Truly! God is my Lord and your Lord, so worship Him.
That is a Straight Path.
The Qur'an,Chapter 3, The People of Imraan, Verse 49-51

And so, the followers of Jesus grew in number, witnessing his miracles and the Truth of the Revelation he taught. On one occasion, his disciples requested another miracle, asking him if God could send down from heaven a table laden with food and drink.

In the Name of God, the Most Gracious, the Most Merciful
Jesus said, "Fear God, if you are indeed believers."
They said: "We only wish to eat from it and satisfy our hearts;
and to know that you have indeed told us the truth;
and that we ourselves may be its witnesses."
Jesus, son of Mary, said, "Oh God, our Lord! Send us from heaven a table set
that there may be for us—for the first and the last of us—a solemn festival
and a sign from You; and provide us with sustenance, for You are the Best
Sustainer (of our needs).
The Qur'an,Chapter 5, The Table, Verses 112-114

God Almighty responded but warned:

I will send it down to you, but if any of you after that disbelieves,
then I will punish him with a torment such as I have not inflicted on any one
among all the mankind and jinn."
The Qur'an,Chapter 5, The Table, Verse 115

Jesus dutifully obeyed his Lord and taught the Truth of the Gospels and the Message of the Prophets before him. However, the Pharisees, who were entrusted with guarding the Laws of Moses, refused to recognize him as the Messiah. Moreover, they were threatened that he preached to all nations, not just the Israelites. Rather than honor Jesus, they rejected and persecuted him and his followers. They sought to kill him by means of crucifixion, but God did not permit a dishonorable death for his beloved Prophet. Instead, He showed the enemies of Jesus a man bearing his likeness, who they crucified in his place. God, the Merciful and All-Compassionate, then raised Jesus to Heaven above, where he resides alive until this day!

And they said (in boast):
"We killed the Messiah Jesus, son of Mary, the Messenger of God."
But they did not kill or crucify him, although it appeared so to them;
and those who differ therein are full of doubts.
They have no certain knowledge:
they follow nothing but conjecture for surely they did not kill him.
For God raised him up unto the Himself.
And God is Ever All-Powerful, All-Wise.
The Qur'an,Chapter 4, The Women, Verses 157-158

The Lord tells us in the Qur'an that there will be a second coming of Jesus the Messiah, who will return at a time when Satan dominates the earth. His return is a sign of the inevitable: The Hour of Judgment when all mankind will be held accountable before God.

"In the Name of God, the Most Gracious, the Most Merciful
And he (Jesus) shall be a Sign (for the coming of) the Hour (of Judgment).
Therefore, have no doubt about it (the Hour of Judgment) and follow Me.
This is the Straight Path (leading to God and the Kingdom of Heaven).
The Qur'an,Chapter 43, The Gold Adornments, Verse 61

At that time, the Antichrist, a false messiah, will lead mankind down a path of wickedness and destruction. A God-fearing man named the Mahdi will oppose him, while guiding believing men, women and children to righteous action. During this war, pitting the forces of good against the forces of evil, Jesus will rest his hands on the wings of two angels and descend from Heaven to a white minaret East of Damascus. He will join in prayer behind the Mahdi and then slay the Antichrist.

After the death of the Antichrist, peace and justice will reign on earth. Jesus and the Mahdi will rule a wonderful worldwhere all mankind exists as one beautiful community where everyone believes in God, submits to His Will and does good deeds. However, this utopia will not last. Satan will order the horrific beasts Gog and Magog to disperse throughout the lands wreaking havoc, carnage and destruction. Thankfully, Jesus will pray to God to destroy them and his prayers will be answered.

The Messiah's reign over the earth will last 40 years, after which he will die and be buried in the vacant grave in Medina next to Prophet Muhammad. His second coming and death are Signs that the Day of

Judgment is nigh. On that day, all of mankind from Adam to the last person born will be assembled before God, the Merciful and All-Compassionate.

The trumpet will be sounded,
when all in the heavens and on earth will swoon,
except those it will please God to exempt.
Then, a second one will be sounded when,
behold, they will be standing looking on!
And the Earth will shine with the glory of its Lord.
The Book of Records will be placed open.
The Prophets and witnesses will be brought forward,
a just decision pronounced between them;
and they will not be wronged in the least.
And every soul will be paid in full for the consequence of its deeds;
and God knows full well what they do.
The disbelievers will come in crowds until,
when they arrive, its gates will be opened.
And its keepers will say,
"Didn't Messengers come to you from among yourselves,
reciting to you the Verses of your Lord
and warning you of this meeting day of yours?
The Qur'an, Chapter 39, The Crowds, Verses 68-71

On the Day of Judgment, the Lord of the Worlds will divide all living creatures into two groups. Those who loved God, followed His Prophets, and did good deeds will be granted eternal bliss in the Gardens of Paradise; and those who disavowed Him, conspired against His Prophets, and enjoined evil will be thrown into the blazing inferno of Hell.

Muhammad (Peace Be Upon Him)

Muhammad (peace be upon him) is not the father of any of your men,
but the Apostle of God and the Seal of the Prophets;
and God has full knowledge of all things.
The Qur'an, Chapter 33, The Confederates, Verse 40

In the year 570, Prophet Muhammad, whose name means "highly praised," was born into the wealthy and powerful tribe of Quraysh in the Arabian Peninsula. His father, Abdullah, died before his birth and so his mother, Aminah, and nursemaid, Halimah, decided to raise him in the desert among camels, goats and sheep. Surrounded by open sky and vast tracts of land, he grew in awe of the greatness of the Creator of the Heavens and the Earth. He had no formal schooling and did not learn to read or write. Yet, everyone recognized Muhammad as a pure and special child.

Aminah died when Muhammad was six years old and he was taken to Mecca to be raised by his grandfather, Abd al Muttalib, a respected elder of the city. Abd al Muttalib loved him dearly and taught him how to counsel people who came to him for help and advice. In this environment, he learned how to communicate with people and resolve their problems wisely and fairly.

When Muhammad was eight, his grandfather died and he went to live with his paternal uncle. Under the guardianship of Abu Talib, who was a merchant and trader, he learned to be a businessman and traveled far and wide across the lands. During a journey to Syria, Abu Talib's caravan stopped for food and rest at the home of Buhayra, a hermit who followed the teachings of Jesus, the Messiah. Buhayra told Abu Talib that the boy was very special indeed, and had the markings of an apostle of God.

As years passed, Prophet Muhammad grew into manhood. He was of medium build and extremely handsome. He had large black eyes with a touch of brown and long, thick eyelashes. He had black wavy hair, a thick black beard and fair complexion. His body was strong and sturdy with long muscular limbs and tapering fingers. His forehead was large and prominent, nose sloping and his cheeks generous. His mouth was somewhat large and he had well-set teeth and a pleasant smile. His gait was firm and swift making it difficult for others to keep pace. His face was kind, but he was often deep in thought and silent for extended periods of time. He always kept busy and did not speak without a purpose; and at times would emphasize a point by repeating it. His laugh was mostly a smile and he kept his emotions under firm control. When annoyed, he would turn aside or keep silent. When pleased, he would lower his eyes.

Muhammad was deeply drawn to God. He constantly contemplated the world around him and was troubled by what he saw. It bothered him that the rich were often arrogant and took advantage of the poor and humble. He tried to settle disputes in a fair manner; and was known for honesty and sincerity in his business dealings and conduct. The people of Quraysh came to trust him so much that he was known as "The Trustworthy."

Muhammad's outstanding character was noticed by Khadijah, a beautiful, wealthy woman 15 years his senior. She needed someone honest and dependable to manage her business affairs and hired him. After some time, she asked him to marry her. They loved and respected each other very much; and it was a beautiful marriage. God gave them two sons: Qasim, who died at the age of two and Abdullah, who died during infancy; and onedaughter: Fatima.

Muhammad would often retreat into the mountains to contemplate the Creator of the Heavens and the Earth and the purpose of existence. One day during the month of Ramadan, when he was 40 years old, he received his first Revelation from God while in the Cave of Hira. The Angel Gabriel told him, "Recite!" He replied, "I cannot recite." The Angel Gabriel embraced him and repeated: "Recite!" Muhammad's answer was the same as before. Gabriel embraced him again and told the Prophet to say the following:

Recite! In the Name of your Lord Who has created (all that exists).
He has created man from a clot (a piece of thick congealed blood).
Recite! And your Lord is the Most Generous.
Who has taught by the pen.
He has taught man what he knew not.
The Qur'an,Chapter 96, The Clot, Verses1-5

Months later, Prophet Muhammad (pbuh) received his second Revelation telling him to spread the Message of Islam.

Oh you (Muhammad) enveloped in garments!
Arise and warn!
And magnify your Lord!
And purify your garments!
And keep away from the idols!
The Qur'an,Chapter 74, The One Enveloped, Verses1 5

At that time, the tribes of Mecca believed in many gods and worshipped idols. In fact, they even engaged in idol worship at the Ka'aba itself, the Holy House of God built by the Prophet Adam and then rebuilt by Prophet Abraham and Prophet Ismail. It was clear that the people of

Quraysh had forgotten that the Lord created them to worship Him and Him Alone. God told Muhammad:

And when they commit an evil deed
(going around the Ka'aba worshipping idols,
sometimes naked committing unlawful acts), they say:
"We found our forefathers doing it and God has commanded it on us."
Say: (Oh Muhammad): "No, God never commands evil. Do you say of God
what you know not?"Say: "My Lord has commanded justice and that you
should face Him only in every place of worship, in prayers, and invoke Him
only making your religion sincere to Him. As He brought you into being, so
shall you be brought into being (on Judgment Day) in two groups: one blessed
and one wretched.
The Qur'an,Chapter 7, The Heights, Verse 28-29

Over a period of 23 years, the Angel Gabriel visited Muhammad often and taught him the entire Revelation of the Qur'an, which the Prophet instructed his companions to write down. Muhammad's mission was to guide mankind to worship God, the Creator and Sustainer of the universe, and to submit to His Will. By testifying that there is only One True God and Muhammad is His Messenger, one submits to God's Will. The religion of submitting to God's Will is called Islam and one who submits is a Muslim.

God! There is no god but He,
the Ever-Living, Eternal and Self-subsisting,
by Whom all is created and subsists.
No slumber can overtake Him or sleep.
All things in the Heavens and on Earth belong to Him.
Who can intercede in His presence except by His permission?
He knows what lies before (His creations) and what is behind them.

*Nor shall they grasp any of His knowledge except that which he permits.
His throne extends over the Heavens and Earth, and He does not tire
guarding and preserving them. And He is the High, the Supreme."*
The Qur'an, Chapter 2, The Cow, Verse 255

Khadijah was the first to embrace Islam, followed by Muhammad's ten-year old cousin Ali IbnAbiTalib. His friend Abu Bakr and his wife and daughters were the next to convert, along withZaydIbnHarithah, who was a slave. Soon, HamzahIbnAbd al Muttalib and Omar Ibn al Khattab embraced Islam and became trusted companions of the Prophet. All accepted Islam by testifying: "There is no deity (worthy of worship) except God (The One True God) and Muhammad is the Messenger of God." Meanwhile, the Prophet continued to share the Qur'an with the people of Quraysh, many of whom were attracted by the justice, wisdom and magnificence of God's Words, which decreed that all people regardless of gender, color, social status or age be treated with dignity and kindness.

At first, the leaders of Quraysh felt threatened. The Ka'aba had become the center for idol worship, which brought much trade and commerce to Mecca. Polytheism was also the religion of their fathers and grandfathers. Thus, they began a campaign to persecute the Muslims and boycotted them from trade and marriage for three years. Some of Muhammad's followers were killed for failing to deny their testimony of faith. Others fled to Ethiopia, which was ruled by a kind and wise Christian king who sheltered them.

These were very difficult years for Prophet Muhammad (pbuh), who was tasked with spreading the Message of Islam in a hostile and resistant environment. His trials became most difficult in the year 620, when his beloved uncle Abu Talib and wife Khadijah died. Later that year, he traveled to the city of Taif to teach its people about Islam. Not only was he scorned, they sent gangs of children and the mentally ill to jeer and throw stones at him. He left Taif in the depths of sadness, humiliation and despair; and took refuge in an orchard. God's beloved Prophet prayed to Him to give him strength, saying:

Oh God, to You I complain of my weakness,
lack of resources and humiliation before these people.
You are the Most Merciful, the Lord of the weak and my Master.
To whom will You send me?
To one estranged, bearing ill will or an enemy given power over me?
If You do not assign me any worth, I care not,
for Your favor is abundant upon me.
I seek refuge in the light of Your Face by which all darkness is dispelled
and every affair of this world and the next is set right,
lest Your anger should descend upon me
or Your displeasure light upon me.
I need only Your pleasure and satisfaction
for only You enable me to do good and evade the evil.
There is no power and no might but You."
Sahih Al Bukhari Collection of
the Sayings and Deeds of Prophet Muhammad

In response to the Prophet's prayer, God sent an angel who offered to crush the city of Taif with the two hills surrounding it. Showing great tolerance, love, mercy and optimism, Muhammad replied:

"No! It is my hope that from their children
will be those who believe in God,
The One, and do not associate anything with Him."
Sahih Al Bukhari Collection of

Muhammad returned to Mecca and, after experiencing his most difficult days, received from His Lord the ultimate comfort and solace. God then took His Messenger on a heavenly journey throughout the night, showing him the secrets of the Heavens:

Glorified be He (God), Who took His slave Muhammadfor a journey by night from the Sacred Mosque (in Mecca) to the Farthest Mosque (in Jerusalem), the neighborhood whereof We have blessed in order that We might show him of Our Signs. Verily, He is the All-Hearer and All-Seer!
The Qur'an, Chapter 17, The Night Journey, Verse 1

Soon after, as Muhammad prayed at the Ka'aba, Angel Gabriel returned with Buraq, a white-winged steed smaller than a mule and bigger than a donkey. The Prophet mounted Buraq and, with lightning speed, they flew across the sky from Mecca to Jerusalem, viewing astounding sights along the way. When they descended upon the Noble Sanctuary, Muhammad tethered Buraq to the wall of the Temple Mount, entered the Farthest Mosque and led the Prophets in prayer. Then, in the company of Angel Gabriel, he ascended through the Heavens greeting Prophets Adam, John, Zechariah, Jesus, Joseph, Enoch, Aaron and Moses on the way, all of whom acknowledged hisProphethood. When he reached the Seventh Heaven, he met Prophet Abraham and was shown the Great Mosque in Heaven, circumambulated by 70,000 angels. Then, he was brought into the light of God's presence at the distance of two bows' length. God revealed to him what He willed and instructed him to teach the believers to pray 50 times a day. On his descent, Prophet Muhammad spoke to Prophet Moses, who told him to return to his Lord to ask for a decrease in number. Greatly embarrassed but urged on by Moses, Muhammad pleaded with God repeatedly until the number of mandatory daily prayers was reduced to five.

When he returned to Mecca, Muhammad told the story of his amazing journey and, as the number of believers grew, so too did the anger of those who rejected his Message. Muslims were threatened with death and all kinds of persecution. Moreover, the clans of Quraysh joined together in a wicked conspiracy to kill the Prophet. Angel Gabriel advised the Prophet to migrate with the Muslims to Yathrib, a city 250 miles to the north Mecca.

At this point, God informed His Prophet of the plan by Quraysh to kill him. The Prophet asked his young cousin Ali ibn Abi Talib, to sleep in his bed and Ali accepted.Meanwhile, Muhammadand Abu Bakr left the city by foot. Traveling under the cover of the darkness of night, they left the city by foot, horse and camel, while taking various routes careful not to be seen or caught. To throw off their enemies, Muhammad and his companionAbuBakr traveled south to the mountain of Thawr, where they hid in a cave for three days. Enemy soldiers found the cave, but God protected them by causing a spider to spin a web over the entrance and a dove to build a nest at its door. The enemies were thus deflected from entering and Muhammad and Abu Bakr were saved.

When the Prophet and his followers arrived in Yathrib, the people greeted him with great enthusiasm. Immediately, he began to build a mosque and Yathrib, under the rule of God's law, came to be known as Al Medina or "The City." To ensure peace, he established a treaty creating a just, equitable and cooperative code of conduct for all its inhabitants – Muslim, Christian and Jewish – regardless of their faith. This migration and the establishment of Medina occurred in the year 622 and mark the start of the Islamic calendar.

In Medina, the Prophet Muhammad continued to receive Revelations, which grew to comprise the basis of a comprehensive system of Holy Law governing all aspects of life. He established "The Five Pillars of Islam" which are: declaring that there is only One God and that Muhammad is His Messenger; praying five times a day; fasting during the month of Ramadan; giving charity; and making the pilgrimage to Mecca.

After the migration to Medina, Islam continued to spread throughout the Arabian Peninsula; and its enemies continued to attack the Prophet. The Battles of Badr, Uhud and the Trench were fought in or around Medina and many of the believers bravely sacrificed their lives to defend the Faith. God told them to remain steadfast as some would never believe.

"In the Name of God, the Most Gracious, the Most Merciful
Say, "Oh disbelievers! I worship not that which you worship.
Nor will you worship that which I worship. And I shall not worship that which
you are worshipping. Nor will you worship that which I worship.
To you be your religion and to me my religion."
The Qur'an, Chapter 109, The Disbelievers

Finally, a year after the Battle of the Trench, Muhammad and 1,500 of his companions left for Mecca to perform the annual pilgrimage to the Ka'aba. They were turned away, but in a stroke of political genius the Prophet signed the Treaty of Hudaybiyah with Quraysh, agreeing to a ten-year truce stating that they could return the following year and thereafter. This treaty created favorable conditions for the Muslims and allowed them to travel in peace.

In the interim, Muhammad sent many companions who had memorized the Qur'an to new lands to spread the Word of God. He also sent letters to the kings of the Byzantine Empire, Persia, Yemen and Abyssinia inviting them to embrace Islam. Swiftly, hundreds and thousands embraced Islam. North, South, East and West, the people of the lands testified, "I witness that there is no deity except God and Muhammad is the Messenger of God."

"In the Name of God, the Most Gracious, the Most Merciful
When there comes God's help and victory,
and you see people joining God's religion in droves,
then celebrate the glory of your Lord and pray for His forgiveness,
for He is Oft-Returning (in grace, compassion and mercy)."
The Qur'an, Chapter 110, The Divine Support

By the year 630, Islam was so widely accepted that when a few of the Quraysh broke the Treaty of Hudaybiyah, the Prophet and 10,000 followers were able to enter Mecca and control it peacefully without a fight. Muhammad circled the Ka'aba seven times while riding a camel and ordered all idols to be destroyed. Once again, monotheism was established in Mecca, as practiced during the times of Prophets Adam, Abraham and Ishmael.

Two years later, Prophet Muhammadmade a farewell pilgrimage to Mecca and delivered his last sermon in the Valley of Arafat outside of the city. On top of a hill, now known as the Mount of Mercy, he spoke to a sea of believers and said:

Oh people, no Prophet or Apostle will come after me
and no new faith will be born.

Reason well, therefore, oh people,
and understand my words which I convey to you.
I leave behind me two things, the Qur'an and my example
theSunnah, and if you follow these you will never go astray."

Prophet Muhammad also admonished racism in any form. He said: "All
mankind is from Adam and Eve. An Arab has no superiority over a non-Arab,
nor does a non-Arab have any superiority over an Arab. Also, a White has no
superiority over a Black, and Black has no superiority over a White except by
piety and gppd action. Learn that every Muslim is a brother to every Muslim
and that the Muslims constitute one brotherhood. Nothing shall be legitimate
to a Muslim which belongs to a fellow Muslim unless it is given freely and
willingly. Do not therefore do injustice to yourselves."
Sahih Al Bukhari Collection of
the Sayings and Deeds of Prophet Muhammad

A few months later, at the age of 63, the Holy Prophet fell ill and
passed from this world.

"In the Name of God, the Most Gracious, the Most Merciful
Surely we belong to God and to Him shall we return."
The Qur'an, Chapter 2, The Cow, Verse 156

Today, he is buried within the massive expanse of the Prophet's
Mosque in Medina. Next to his grave, there is an empty tomb that awaits
Jesus the Messiah. Muhammad, peace be upon him, was the Seal of the
Prophets, who delivered the Message in its final form. Like those before him,
he taught that our purpose in life is to worship God.

*"In the Name of God, the Most Gracious, the Most Merciful
O ye who believe! Believe in God and his Apostle, and the scripture which He
hath sent to His Apostle and the scripture which He sent to those before (him).
Any who denieth God, His Angels, His Books, His Apostles and the Day of
Judgment, hath gone far, far astray."*
The Qur'an, The Women, Verse 136

In the Name of God, the Most Gracious, the Most Merciful

"Say: He is God, the One and Only!

God, the Eternal, Absolute, Self-sufficient Master,

He begets not, nor was He begotten,

And there is none equal or comparable to Him."

The Qur'an, The Purity, Verses 1-4

ALLAH

By: Zaynab Khalfan

*A*ppreciate Allah for the Qur'an that has guided us

*L*ive by the Qur'an He sent down

*L*ove Him for the creations He has given us

*A*mazing things only happen with the help of Allah

*H*ave patience and Allah will always be with you

Notes

Notes

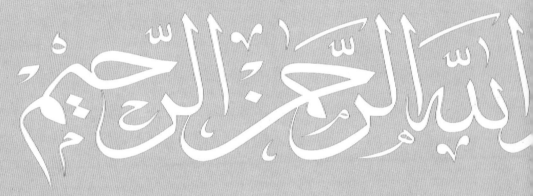

بسم الله الرحمن الرحيم

In the name of God, Mos